Acclaim for *The Spiral of Creativity*

"One of the enduring metaphors of the American experience is the upward spiral of progress. One of the enduring metaphors of the *human* experience is the spiral of creativity. Join Brecia Kralovic-Logan in *The Spiral of Creativity* as she teaches you how to increase and sustain your creativity and live a truly spirited creative life!"
— Eric Maisel, author of *Coaching the Artist Within, Fearless Creating* and *Secrets of a Creativity Coach*

"In *The Spiral of Creativity*, Brecia, the masterful artist that she is, has designed a series of creative adventures for your spirit to spark your inner creative expression and expand you as a person. It is a treasure chest of activities written by a prolific and successful creative woman. So clear off your workspace and let Brecia guide you deeper into your creative brilliance."
— Gail McMeekin, author of *The 12 Secrets of Highly Creative Women* and *The 12 Secrets of Highly Successful Women*

"I feel such gratitude for having met you, and experienced firsthand the gentle, profound depth of your wisdom, your compassionate & graceful teaching ability...your 'Art-Fullness'."
— Sedona Vigliotta

THE SPIRAL OF
CREATIVITY

To JoAnna

THE SPIRAL OF
CREATIVITY

Mastering the Art of a Spirited Life

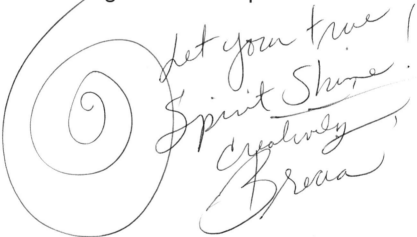

Let your true Spirit Shine! Creatively, Brecia

BRECIA KRALOVIC-LOGAN

pebble in the pond books
Santa Barbara, CA

pebble in the pond books
3905 State St. #7-243,
Santa Barbara, CA 93105

First Edition

Printed in the United States of America.

Library of Congress Control Number: 2014904386

Publisher's Catologing-In-Publication

Kralovic-Logan, Brecia.

    The spiral of creativity : mastering the art of a spirited life / Brecia Kralovic-Logan. -- 1st ed. -- Santa Barbara, CA : Pebble in the Pond Books, c2014.

    p. ; cm.

      ISBN: 978-0-9916325-1-0
      Summary: Using the powerful, ancient, symbol of the spiral, the author coaches the reader through the five essential elements for discovering their own creative resources, vast intuitive powers, and individual spirit: Spirited, Passionate, Intuitive, Real, Authentic, Life choices. Includes hands on art activities, writing exercises, guided imagery, and spiral meditations to help the reader explore their own unique strengths and challenges.--Publisher.

      1. Creative ability. 2. Spirals. 3. Intuition. 4. Self-realization. 5. Conduct of life. 6. Spiritual life. I. Title.

BF408 .K73 2014   2014904386
153.3/5--dc23   1404

Book and Publishing Consultant: Ellen Reid
Cover and Interior Design: Lynda Rae
Author Photo: Natasha Logan

This book is dedicated to my amazing husband George, out-of-the-box thinker extraordinaire; and my adored children Nikolas, Natasha, and Tatiana, who ultimately are my greatest teachers and guides.

What a team!
Love, love, love

Contents

An Invitation

*"Sometimes questions are more
important than answers."*

Nancy Willard

C reativity is what makes you feel fully alive. It's your
spirit's sweet power source. Tuning into it, you discover
that you are a vibrating bundle of curiosity, imagination,
and wonder. You feel an exciting sense of expansion and
possibilities. When you embrace it, nurture it and claim it
as your own, you find that you are able to create a life that
you love. If only you knew how to access that creative part
of you more fully and more often.

Now is the time to pay attention to that urge to connect
with your creativity.

The Spiral of Creativity calls you to embrace your own
amazing inner resources and bring into being the dreams
that are waiting to "complete you." Would you like to infuse
more of your true creative spirit into every part of your life,
your relationships, and your work? By following the spiral,
you will be propelled straight to the heart of who you really
are now and who you want to become. Perhaps you have
encountered Joseph Campbell's famous invitation to "follow
your bliss." Yes! Are you ready for your very own bliss-fest?

Your creative nature is like a kid sitting poised at the
top of the slide. You eagerly wait for the rush of the ride.
You want to feel the wind in your face and the thrill in
your gut. But you just might need a little nudge to get

going. Don't worry. You are not alone. As a creativity coach, I have designed this book to support you through the most common obstacles that we as creative humans find ourselves entangled with, including our reluctance to recognize our own creativity. Learn to let go of the thoughts and ideas that have held you back and let your spirited life flow and flourish.

Mastering the art of your spirited life opens the door to your limitless power to express your true self. Yes, there will be challenges. But self-awareness will become your most effective tool for change. As you complete the activities in this book, you will experience the freedom and insight that comes with self-knowledge and you will grow into your own creative spirit in all its glory.

Imagine sparklers on the Fourth of July—you know, the ones that send out hundreds of tiny, bright specks of light exploding into the darkness. Picture yourself standing with a sparkler in each hand and with your arms stretching wide open. Wave your sparklers in ever-expanding circles and draw giant spiraling light trails all around yourself. Feel the sparkling energy surge through you as if the light is shooting right straight from your heart, out into the night sky. Now get ready to generate sparks of your own.

The timing is right, the stars are lined up, and you are poised to play, to write, to think, to feel, to discover and to create your beautiful, exciting life of joyful purpose.

Let *The Spiral of Creativity* be your guide. Are you ready to begin?

BRECIA KRALOVIC-LOGAN

2

How to Use This Guidebook

"Walking the Spiral.
Return again, return again.
Return to the land of your soul.
Return to what you are. Return to who you are.
Return to where you are.
Born and born again, return again."

Rafae

The symbol of the spiral, with its pulsing, almost palatable energy will be our dynamic metaphor and will accompany us through the activities in this book that will support our continual creative expansion. The chapters, inspired by the word "spiral" as an acronym — SPIRAL — guide us through our Spirited, Passionate, Intuitive, Real, Authentic, Life choices. The spiral provides us with a pathway for exploring both the exciting and the challenging elements that we will encounter while creating a life that we love.

This is not going to be a linear process. We will be repeatedly circling back to incorporate accumulated insights from previous chapters. Our spiral path becomes a natural net of self-knowledge, a quilt of light to wrap ourselves in, and a woven web of wonders. Our spiraling inward and spiraling outward will become a rhythm, a song, a dance, and our spirited, creative life.

There are simple ways we can access our inner places — those that we are not even conscious of, but that are an essential part of our being. They are the part of us that responds to images, rituals, symbols, dreams, poetry, acronyms and metaphors. You will find all of these in this book and many opportunities for you to add your own ideas. You will be invited continually to connect your spirited creativity with your passionate energy. Using your senses you will check in with your body sensations.

Each chapter offers four ways to help you explore new areas of growth, and to open you to novel possibilities for expressing your individual creativity:

1. Shine On writing prompts

2. Create to Relate hands-on activities

3. A Spiral Activity based on the spiral symbol

4. An Affirmation example and the opportunity to write your own

The Shine On writing prompts and the Create to Relate activities are your best tools for exploring your personal passions and power, so you will find them offered through-out the chapters. The Spiral Activity gives you a chance to play with our central symbol, which connects you directly to your inner source. The Affirmation that appears at the end of each chapter might be a tool that you will want to incorporate into your daily spirited life practice.

Shine On

You will find Shine On writing prompts in each chapter that offer you the opportunity to explore your thoughts and feelings about the material presented in each section. These awareness activities are coaching tools designed to help you "shine a light" on a specific facet of your creative life. Each question leads you along the path that spirals inward, bringing awareness to your unique strengths, passions, gifts, fears and challenges. Remember that your awareness is an essential tool for change.

By writing out your thoughts and feelings you will become aware of your true spirit. Plan to spend time doing each writing exercise. It is a good idea to have a journal that you can keep private in addition to this guidebook. You might like to decorate your journal with spirals and keep it somewhere where only you will access it.

Create to Relate

"Create, create, so you can relate
to ideas in a state that helps you await
the unique trait that will inflate
your great Imagination."
BRECIA KRALOVIC-LOGAN

These hands-on creative activities are designed to help you integrate the concepts in each chapter by incorporating them into a tangible, physical experience. All of the activities will have suggestions of how to engage your senses to integrate your inner wisdom into your outward expression of creative individuality. Here is where you will bring your personal style into play, working in the ways that feel right for you. You may want to draw, dance, sing, perform, or cook something from your garden in order to bring your thoughts, ideas, and feelings more fully into your daily life. Then when you get to Chapter Five you can develop these activities into the daily choices that become your spirited life.

Really allow yourself to play with these activities. Create as big as you want. Get large pads of newsprint, binders and boxes, poster board whatever supplies feel right to you. Gather up your color-makers: pencils, pens, markers, crayons, paints, pastels etc and create a space for them somewhere where they are easily accessible, preferable where you can see them. Collect a stack of old magazines to glean images from. Set up your phone or computer with your favorite music. Be ready to hunt through your spice cupboard for colors and textures, or to rearrange your outdoor space to express your desired movement.

Spiral Activity

The Spiral Activities incorporate this powerful symbol as an activator to rev up our intuitive engines. Let the image of this ancient symbol speak to you and charge your creative growth. You will find a large spiral image designed especially for this activity at the end of each chapter. You can also download the spiral images from the web site. Experiment with using the spiral to create a variety of visual reminders to accompany your writing and creating exercises.

Affirmations

Affirmations are, simply put, positive energy thoughts. They connect us with our power source of love. They project our good out in front of us and propel us toward it. You will find an Affirmation at the end of each chapter, along with an opportunity for you to create your own. Don't worry if this is new to you. There is more about how to write and use affirmations in Chapter One.

Let *The Spiral of Creativity* be your springboard and inspiration. There are no one-size-fits-all solutions to creative challenges, so feel free to adapt and play with what works best for you. Your creative process may parallel the experiences of others, but you have your own unique style and self-knowledge leads to creative expansion. You may use this guidebook over and over again on your personal spiral journey. Let your senses guide your imagination. Have fun!

The Importance of Awareness

*"What is necessary to change a person is
to change his awareness of himself."*
ABRAHAM MASLOW

Throughout this guidebook, you will be urged to bring your awareness to various aspects of your creative life. When we are asked to "shine a light on" something, we are being asked to bring our attention, our focus, our feelings, and even our unconscious attention to that thing. We are trying to get a clear perspective, to see it from different angles, to get to know it from the inside out.

The awareness that we are called to use while we explore the spiral of creativity is a total awareness. It involves a deep kind of seeing that requires a collaboration of mind, heart and spirit. This means that we need to go beyond just what we think because our thoughts can sometimes lead us astray.

Let me share a story that illustrates this:

A few years back, I was the president of an art organization in Los Angeles. To get everyone's attention I would bring my Tibetan bowl with me and give it a tap to start the meeting. The lovely resonant sound of the bowl would settle everyone into the mode of listening. One month I was preparing to drive down to Los Angeles for the meeting and I couldn't find the bowl. I searched high and low. I thought that perhaps I had left the bowl at the meeting location the month before. I was really hoping to find it when I arrived but after looking everywhere, I became resigned to thinking that it was gone. I convinced myself that I had left it and it was now lost forever. I felt sad and disappointed that I had lost my bowl and its beautiful resonant sounds.

One day, weeks later, I walked into my studio, and there on a shelf just at my eye level was my Tibetan bowl. I had been walking past it in plain view every day for weeks! My mind had been so convinced that I had lost it, that I actually stopped seeing it. I was shocked to find it sitting in such an obvious spot especially when I "knew" that I had lost it. I marveled at the power my mind had over my ability to see what was literally right in front of me.

You will find that the activities in this book will be constantly guiding you to pay close attention to your physical sensations, your feelings, and your intuition in addition to what you are thinking. The rituals, guided imagery, art making and use of symbols encourages you to use even those parts of you that are not a part of your conscious thought processes.

Awareness becomes our key and our gateway to creating the life we love. However, awareness is just the beginning. It is the life choices we make that will lead to mastering our spirited life. Throughout this guidebook you will have opportunities to bring your full awareness to the wholeness of your creativity. You will discover the choices that support your true way of being fully alive.

You have already stepped onto the path. Embracing the interactivity of this book will set you in motion. Explore each facet of your creativity. Bring your curiosity out to play. Open your heart and let your spirit shine.

Chapter One

Spiraling into Our Creativity

*"What is art but life upon the larger scale…
graduating up in a spiral line of expanding and
ascending gyres, it pushes toward the intense
significance of all things hungry for the infinite."*

ELIZABETH BARRETT BROWNING

When you picked up *The Spiral of Creativity* you were following the urge for more joy, more satisfaction and a sense of growing into a life you love. You are spirited. You are passionate. You are intuitive and you are creative. Creativity is a way of seeing, feeling and thinking and you can discover how this translates into your unique expression in the world in your work, in your play, in your close relationships and in your role within your greater community.

When I first started teaching creativity workshops using the spiral as a tool, my son asked me, "When you are talking about the spiral, are you talking about spiraling in or spiraling out?"

Nik's question zeroed in on the movement and energy inherent in the spiral. As we make our way through this guidebook, we will be spiraling inward to shine a light on our unique strengths and qualities, bringing our awareness to all that makes us who we are. Then the creative process will take us spiraling outward toward the expression of our individuality and spirited creativity. This continual action of spiraling in and out synergizes our life choices and infuses our days with thousands of sparkling moments.

It's no wonder that the image of the spiral has been found in so many varied cultures to symbolize human growth from birth to death. The flow of the spiral is all around us in nature, from the expansive galaxies to the structure of our own DNA. Spirals fascinate and inform us on many levels, from physics and astronomy, to religion and witchcraft. *The Spiral of Creativity* invites us to play with this ancient symbol as both a tool and a pathway for self-discovery and creative living.

We will follow this pathway through the chapters which are named for each letter of the acronym SPIRAL: Spirited, Passionate, Intuitive, Real, Authentic, and Living. In this way, the word itself becomes our multifaceted guide. By design, we will circle back around to the previous chapters, revisiting the information and self-explorations in an organic cycle that tunes into the rhythmic nature of our lives and of our environment. We will travel the spiral pathway inward and outward, over and over again. Like inhaling and exhaling, our expanding and exploring will take on a natural rhythm.

SHINE ON

Your Relationship with the Spiral Symbol

Use the following questions as writing prompts to help you to explore your thoughts and feelings about the spiral. You may want to conjure an image of the spiral as you write, or visualize a sparkling spiral of light as you answer these questions:

1. What is my relationship to the ancient symbol of the spiral?

2. Does it have any place in my life at the moment?

3. What meaning does it invoke for me?

4. When I think about the term "spiraling out of control" do I have any negative associations with the word "spiral?"

When I started writing this book I began to notice spirals everywhere I looked. My studio was filled with artwork from dozens of different artists that incorporated the spiral. I really wasn't even aware of the fact that I was surrounded by so many variations of spirals. From the shells I collected at the beach to the wind chimes hanging near my door, spirals have become an integral part of my environment. I invite you to begin noticing the spiral images around you as you go through your day.

CREATE TO RELATE
1000+ Spirals

As we embrace the spiral as our muse, we are going to be creating dozens of ways to use the symbol and incorporate it into our spirited, creative lives. This first activity is one that we can continue to use on an ongoing basis. It can be used as a playful meditation, keeping our conscious mind happily busy while allowing space for our inner guidance to emerge or for a peaceful calm to settle in. We may find that creating spirals allows us to think through a problem more clearly, or it may let us drift into a daydream that has been waiting for an opening to appear as an inspiration. We can use this as a one-minute centering exercise or take all the time we want to luxuriate in the color and curvature of what we are creating.

Look over the choices listed here for creating spirals to see which ones fit you the best. You can choose one method to work with and/or try them all.

You will need:

Paper: Any kind will do. It can be colored or plain, lined or not. You may want to use recycled paper. All of your rejects from the printer, old newspapers, envelopes from bills, all will work fine. Or you may like to use index cards, which have a nice sturdy feel.

Color-makers: Crayons, pencils, markers, pens, pastels, charcoal, watercolors, or acrylics and brushes.

SPIRALS METHOD I

Cut a stack of paper into four-inch squares. (The size is just a suggestion.) Make *lots* of squares at one time, so that you have a stack of at least 100 squares to start with. Use a paper cutter, if you have one, to make the cutting go quickly or use scissors, which are portable and can make the actual cutting a part of the meditation. If you use index cards cut into four-inch squares, you are all set.

- Find a spot that is comfortable for you and set out your color makers.

- Draw or paint a spiral on each square.

- Alternate between starting your spiral drawing in the center of the square and going outward or beginning at the outside edge of the paper and spiraling into the center point.

- Play with the speed and the rhythm of your drawings.

- Use just one color, play with two colors, or layer on multiple colors and media.

- Decorate the background of your spiral drawing and/or embellish the spiral itself with color and texture.

- Alternate hands as you draw and notice any differences you experience while using your non-dominant hand.

- Practice slowly inhaling as you draw one spiral and then slowly exhaling while you draw the next one.

Keep the spiral cards that you make. You can slip them into a zip-top bag or find a box to house them in. You will find new ways to use them introduced later in the book. Keep ten to twelve of your favorite squares close at hand for an activity coming up in the next section on creativity.

SPIRALS METHOD 2

On a large piece of paper, draw spirals. Don't think, just draw. And listen. Choose a place on your paper to begin and then continue drawing until the whole paper is filled.

This method becomes a meditation, a means for occupying your hands and conscious mind so that glimmers of your inner light can shine on through. This can be a good exercise to do when you are trying to solve a problem, make a connection, or follow an idea into its future form. Relax and give yourself over completely to drawing.

Here are some more suggestions to add to the ones above for varying your experience:

- Choose to space the spirals randomly on the page or create an order that pleases you.

- Create spirals in varying sizes from teeny tiny to the size of a whole page.

- Overlap your spirals.

- Create a pathway of spirals across, down, or around the page. You can make a spiral of spirals.

- Make continuous spirals, keeping your color-maker connected to the paper at all times.

- Experiment with using pieces of paper of different colors, textures, and sizes.

- Listen to different kinds of music while playing with your spirals and let that influence the rhythm of your spiral making.

You can use this method on separate sheets of paper of any size, which gives you the opportunity to work in larger formats. You may also use this method in a notebook or in a journal. Make it portable and keep it in your car, or carry it with you to use throughout the day. Don't think of this as an art project with a specific end result. Instead, allow the activity of drawing the spirals and then applying colors and textures to free up your mind.

Play with your spiral-making as an ongoing way of slipping into the zone of imagination, free association, and curious listening. You will want to spiral back to this activity when you are exploring Chapter Four on your intuitive self.

What is Creativity?

*"Creativity is the marriage
humanity makes with eternity."*

Eric Maisel

What comes to your mind when you hear the word "creative?" Is living a creative life something that you value, something that you identify with? Do you see yourself as a creative person? Have you been dancing to your own tune all along? Got your own drum?

Perhaps you grew up believing that your sister was "the creative one" and that you somehow missed the day when they were passing out the creativity juice. Or have you always suspected that there was creative potential in the mix but you just weren't sure how to coax it out?

Creativity is an inherent part of being human. We are all creative. We don't have to spend years as a professional artist, or even produce any kind of "art" at all, to claim our creative powers. The truth is, we are creating our lives every moment of every day whether we know it or not. It's when you become aware of what you are creating and how the process works that you empower yourself to make fulfilling choices.

The essence of creativity is that we are moving from the known to the unknown. We are bringing into being something that did not previously exist. That may be an idea for a new wearable art product line, an innovative design for a new phone app, or a way of getting grandma's wheelchair into the back of our Volkswagen. Either our daily choices will keep us rooted in the comfortableness of what we already know, or we will embrace our creative nature and stretch past our limited thinking as we explore new possibilities.

※

SHINE ON

What Does Creativity Mean to Me?

Let's begin by taking a look at what creativity means to you. You may want to settle into a quiet spot to think and write, or you may prefer to take a walk outdoors. Creativity is the topic. Choose to do one minutes worth of spontaneous free-flowing associations, or take the "crock pot" approach and let your creativity simmer all day long. Either way, in your journal write down every word that comes to mind when you think about creativity. Feel free to include feelings, concepts, qualities, and sensations whatever comes to you. There are no right or wrong answers. If one word won't convey the meaning, use a phrase. There's no need to write an essay. Think more of a list.

Here is a list of "creativity" words compiled from many of my workshops. Chances are you will have some of these words on your list too. Notice that many different feelings and sensations are represented here. We are going for the full circle or whole picture, so please add any words that resonate for you to this list.

Wonder	Awe
Curiosity	Joy
Fulfillment	Wholeness
Satisfaction	Power
Risk	Voice
Appreciation	Imagination
Childlikeness	Newness
Knowledge	Learning
Fear	Freedom
Expansion	Inspiration
Meditative	Source
Beauty	Experimentation
Sensuality	Originality
Versatility	Possibility
Intuition	Facing the Unknown
Light	Connection
Flow	Self-Expression
Self-Awareness	Gratitude
Playfulness	Creating Original Work
Hope	Energy
Fun	Being Present to the Moment
Peacefulness	Letting Go of Perfectionism

Read through this list and say each word out loud. Or better yet, have someone else read the list to you so you can close your eyes and pay close attention to how your body reacts to each word. Notice which words register with you physically and put a mark by those words or highlight them with a colorful marker. Go back and read those words again: they have significant power and can help to guide you. Choose ten to twelve of the words that seem to click with you the most and use them for the activity below. Exploring these concepts will shine a light on what has a charge for you.

Creativity Spiral Cards

You will need:

Cards: Ten to twelve of your favorite four-inch cards (the ones you created with the spirals on them) If you are using recycled paper, choose cards that are relatively clear on the back, as you will be writing on that side this time around.

Color-makers: Crayons, pencils, markers, pens, pastels, charcoal, watercolors or acrylics and brushes.

Print or write one of the creativity words that you chose on each card. Now you have a set of Creativity Cards that you can use for self-discovery along the spiral pathway. Feel free to add on as many of the words from your list that you want to. Most likely, every word that you wrote on your list holds meaning for you. Make as many Creativity Cards as you like.

Creative Seeing, Feeling, and Thinking

"A dream is your creative vision for your life. You must break out of your current comfort zone and become comfortable with the unfamiliar and the unknown."

DENIS WAITLEY

Our creative energy begins with our unique way of being in the world; the way we open ourselves to all that is around us, and the way we honor our feelings and monitor our thoughts. As creative people we experience a full and rich awareness of our selves, and of the world around us. We are curious, open, and willing to risk entering into the unknown.

Does that sound like you? Well, it *is* you. You have the capacity to question, to wonder, to travel the creative pathway inward and to shine a light on all that makes you the amazing individual that you are. You can make choices based on your curious nature, your unique talents and your strengths. You can embrace the risky unknown factors, meeting the challenges that they present to you. You can manifest the scrumptious possibilities that you can dream up for yourself.

Following the spiral pathway inward to clarify our way of seeing, feeling, and thinking is essential for our ongoing expansion into the creative life that we imagine for ourselves.

SHINE ON

Speed Date Your Way to Self-Discovery

Here is a fun way to get familiar with your current paradigm about your creativity. Use this game to get your thoughts flowing freely. Spread your creativity cards out on the table with the spiral image facing up and the words facing down. Randomly choose two cards and quickly look at the words on them. Pair them together to create a statement that reflects your creative experience. Be open to whatever connections occur to you. Be spontaneous. Be yourself. Then move quickly onto the next pair of cards.

Here is an example: If I picked up the cards with "Risk" and "Hope" I might come up with the following statements:

"Every time I start something new, I hope that I won't have to risk stretching beyond my comfort zone but inevitably, I do, and then I am amazed at what I accomplish."

"Sometimes I'm afraid to risk even hoping that I will succeed."

You also can use the card pairs as a prompt for deeper writing. Choosing the cards randomly and in pairs gives you a new perspective and stimulates new ways of seeing and thinking. Write down the pairs and let them inspire you to explore the nooks and crannies of your inner creative landscape.

Creative Risk

"Your joy is your sorrow unmasked.
And the selfsame well from which your laughter
rises was oftentimes filled with your tears.
And how else can it be?
The deeper that sorrow carves into your
being, the more joy you can contain."
FROM *THE PROPHET* BY KAHIL GIBRAN

In the introduction of this book, I asked you to imagine spiraling around waving a lit sparkler. I invited you to imagine the contrast of the fiery, white light blazing against the jet-black night sky so that you could feel a certain excitement. Now, let's focus on the fact that the stick is on fire and the sparks will get progressively closer to your hand. This is risky business. There is a definite tension between creating beautiful visual effects and the risk of getting burned.

How does this relate to our creativity? Although the sparkler analogy is far from perfect, it opens us up to the idea that creative pursuits involve risk. In the above scenario, we pretty much know what the danger is. But in our creative work, we experience different kinds of risk such as the risk of not knowing how something is going to turn out, or the risk that we might make a mess or a mistake. We might also feel the risk that what we create will not hold any meaning for ourselves, or for others once it's completed.

After all, this is the very essence of creativity: facing the unknown. Becoming familiar with the thoughts and emotions associated with risk helps us to learn about ourselves in a way that completes our whole experience of creativity. When we open ourselves to our full range of emotions and thoughts, both the productive ones and the limiting ones, we become aware of what serves to move us ahead toward our desired way of being and what is holding us back. Spirited living is an ongoing process of growth that involves this tension of opposites.

Looking at opposing feelings and thoughts can help us to uncover new perspectives and see a more complete picture of our true spirit. As we examine our feelings around our creativity, we may discover that we have omitted feelings or thoughts that make us uncomfortable or we may have focused on our fears rather than our strengths. We may discover that we often hold opposing thoughts and feelings simultaneously. Our job is to shine a light on all of our internal activity, patiently get familiar with it, kindly accept it all, and willingly choose to act on the thoughts and feelings that serve to move us in the direction that we ultimately desire.

SHINE ON

Tea Party / Part One

Pick a card from your deck of Creativity Cards. Read it out loud. Now think of what the opposite of that word would be and state that out loud. Write down both words.

Now imagine that those two words were having a tea party. What would they say to each other?

Example: If I chose the word "Flow" from my deck, I might choose the word "Stagnation" as it's opposite. If Flow and Stagnation were having a tea party conversation, it might be something like this:

Flow: So, Stag. May I call you Stag? How are you?

Stag: I'm just the same. I don't seem to move at all these days. I've been getting more and more stuck. I think I'm beginning to smell! How about you?

Flow: Oh, I'm moving along quite nicely. I am always on the go, not in a chaotic or frenzied way, mind you. I feel peaceful and calm and I'm enjoying moving in the direction I desire. More Tea?

And so on…

Now it's your turn. Get out the scones. Pour some tea. Pick a card and invite the opposites to sit down and chat. What do these two concepts have to teach you? Continue the dialog until you feel that you have thoroughly explored each word. Listen from your heart. Our goal is to bring awareness to every part of our selves. Self-knowledge supports our spirited life.

※

SHINE ON

Tea Party / Part Two

After your tea party, you will have a new list of words that are the opposites of those in your Creativity Deck. These words are also power-packed and full of emotion and information for us. Settle yourself in and get comfortable before you do this exercise. You may want to actually pour yourself some tea, grab a cookie, put on your favorite slippers and just get really cozy. You may want to light a sweet-smelling candle or build a fire in the fireplace. Call your dog over to sit at your feet. Create a feeling of safety and ease. Breathe and center yourself.

Now you are going to generate a list of feelings that are the opposites of most of the words on your Creativity Cards. Try to be a curious observer. Think of this as a game rather than a place to poison all that is good and positive about creativity.

What feelings are you hoping that your creativity will help you to move through? What judgments, criticisms and labels can you come up with that may have been a part of your thinking and feeling along your way, that you would like to acknowledge, accept and diffuse of their negative influence? Write down every word that comes up.

Here are some of the things that I wrote down on my list:

1. Lethargic
2. Uninspired
3. Tired
4. Depleted
5. Dull
6. Bored
7. Fussy
8. Upset
9. Scared
10. Confused
11. Lost
12. Frustrated
13. Unworthy
14. Overwhelmed

15. Unsure
16. Unvalidated
17. Angry
18. Silly
19. Ridiculous
20. Low/blue
21. Panicked
22. Anxious
23. Worried
24. Unappreciated
25. Isolated
26. Blank
27. Stagnant
28. Doubtful

These thoughts and emotions accompany me as I travel my creative path. They are very real and they give me the opportunity to learn about myself. I am constantly relearning to accept them and love them as a part of who I am. They offer me the challenge of being whole and of seeing clearly all of the possibilities that I have to choose from. My job is to choose not to give them the power to hold me back.

Your list is going to help you to shine a light on all of the varied parts of you. The art of mastering our spirited life involves acknowledging our full range of rich and diverse emotions. Some of our emotions fill us with a sense of expansion and some have the effect of contraction. We actually experience this physically in our bodies, so it makes sense to bring our awareness to the physical sensations of what we feel.

I highly recommend checking into Raphael Cushnir's book, *The One Thing Holding You Back: Unleashing the Power of Emotional Connection* to learn more about feeling your emotions in a physical way. His way of working with expansion and contraction centers your feelings in your body and emphasizes riding out a negative emotion so that you feel it to it's fullest. Then you can accept that emotion as a part of you and it will not prevent you from progressing toward your goals and desires.

He suggests a simple experiment: Hold your arms out wide on either side of you and stretch them outward in an expansive way. Now try to feel sad or angry. It's difficult to do. Alternatively, he suggests that you contract yourself into a small inward shape with your arms wrapped tightly around you. Then try to feel happiness and joy. Again, you can see how closely your physical posture is related to your emotional experience. In your spiral journey you will experience both contraction and expansion. The more you are tuned into your true spirit, the more you will be able to accept your whole self and choose to expand into the dreams that you hold for yourself.

When we deny our emotions or try to shut them out, we set ourselves up for unnecessary tensions that can challenge us in every aspect of our lives. Our health, relationships and our work may all be affected. Thich Nhat Hanh, peace activist and Vietnamese Zen Buddhist monk, talks about bringing acceptance to our feelings of anger. He suggests that we hold our anger as if it was a baby. He encourages us to hold those feelings gently, listen to them closely, and love them dearly. The idea is to be OK with our humanity while we strive to center ourselves in our beautiful individual spirit. Once we become aware of all of our different feelings we can shower ourselves with acceptance and love.

CREATE TO RELATE

Acceptance Ritual

We can approach self-acceptance in many different ways. Rituals are one way that we can bypass our conscious language, and connect with our soul or spirit because rituals engage us on many different levels: physically, emotionally and spiritually. Let this activity speak to you at a soul level.

You will need:
A dozen small smooth stones
A plate
A candle

Put the candle in the middle of the plate. Pick up a stone and feel its weight in your hand. Say the name of one of the emotions that makes you feel contracted. Place the stone on the plate at the base of the candle. Breathe as you release it from your hand. Notice the way you inhale and exhale. Continue placing stones until you have gone through your list.

Now light the candle and watch the flame expand into a full glow. Close your eyes and smell the flame. Feel the warmth. See in your imagination the stones with the light flickering out over them. Open your eyes. Watch how the light dances over the pile of stones, highlighting some, creating shadows, changing as the candle flickers. Be with this scene without thinking. When you are done, blow out the candle. Place this plate somewhere where you can see it often. Repeat the ritual as desired.

Journaling as an Act of Self-Empowerment

*"Journal writing
is a voyage to the interior."*
CHRISTINA BALDWIN

Why do creative people journal? What makes the process of writing down our thoughts and feelings in a notebook so valuable? A journal can be our place to dance with all of our shadowy thoughts and feelings. We can use our journal as a private and safe place to vent, as well as to listen to our own wise counsel.

This is where we get to experience our full range of emotions. We can throw the emotions that we consider to be the most toxic down on the page and have a good look at them. We can see them, feel them, own them, and accept them. We can allow them to teach us something of value and then we can move on. We may find that we have some good insights after a nasty rant. The act of listening to all of our thoughts and feelings, writing them down and validating them holds a great deal of power. This activity makes space for new and transforming thoughts to enter in.

How is this different from complaining or whining? Our journal entries are for our eyes only. We won't verbalize or share these entries with anyone. This is a private party. We invite every part of us to show up and, as the gracious host, we make space for all who arrive. We let every part of us have a say. Then, we get to choose the thoughts and feelings that we want to engage with, knowing that we don't have to dance with every one of them.

SHINE ON

SHINE ON

Journaling Our Wholeness

Here is a simple guided imagery to help you settle into your writing.

You can down load an mp3 audio file of this activity from *The Spiral of Creativity* web site.

Breathe. Imagine the spiral. Slowly trace it with your minds eye into the center, your center. Enter into your calm. Notice your expansion each time you inhale, the contraction when you exhale and the rhythm that your breathing creates. Be aware of the way your body is accepting the flow of calmness with each breath. Let the calmness wash over you. In this flow allow your self to open up and join in the current of calmness. Let your words spill out onto the page. Let this flow of words cleanse you of your fussiness, wash away your hopelessness, carry away your self-doubt and uplift you, buoyant and light and whole.

Use the following writing prompts:

1. How am I feeling today?

2. What, if anything is bothering me?

3. Is there anything that seems to be hindering my progress?

4. What needs my attention? What do I want to change or tweak?

Open your journal and spew it all out onto the page. Don't judge. Keep writing. Respond to your feelings and ask for more information. Fill in everything that is going on with you. Allow each emotion to have its say on the page. When you feel that you have all of your feelings written down you can begin to recognize the dance of all of your emotions.

Choose the feelings that validate you. Find a place for gratitude and even add in some humor. Clarify which attributes, qualities, values, and feelings that you want to carry into the day. Let any limiting or contracting feelings stay on the pages while you cultivate the expansive feelings. Call your attention to your love center before you close the journal and put it in a safe place.

SPIRAL ACTIVITY

Spiral Texture Rub

Have you ever lost your car keys and thought about all of the places they could be? You retrace your steps, thinking of each possible place that you might have set them down. You search but still, can't find them anywhere. Your thoughts are circling around all of the possible scenarios of what happened. Then when you finally give up the search, you find them in some random place that you would never have thought to look. This scenario has happened to me many times.

When I can't find something I'm looking for, I purposefully pay attention to my whole brain. I have learned that I can facilitate a shift from my language-oriented thinking to my visual and spatial thinking by simply choosing to switch from the left side of my brain to the right side. I ask my left-brain to step aside and I invite my right-brain to take over. Then I try to clear my mind of all of the thoughts about where I have been and where the missing article might be. I simply move about my usual routine, paying close attention to any urges I feel to move toward something. I have found things that were "lost" in the strangest places, places I would never have thought to look, in a relatively short amount of time using this method.

When I was growing up, my mother told me that she would pray to Saint Anthony to help her find things that she had lost. She swore that he always came through for her. I believe that giving the task over to this saint, allowed my mom's own intuitive and spatial powers to step up and bypass her thinking. She and I had different ways of achieving the same goal: to allow what was hidden, to be revealed.

For this first spiral activity we are going to use texture and color as our language rather than words. In this way we can activate our spatially oriented right brain as well as our deeper awareness that is not language-oriented. We will be engaging parts of ourselves that we might not actively use as often. We are inviting a new awareness to reveal what might be hidden to us.

Using crayons helps us to find a childlike openness and curiosity. This activity is true play. It helps us to center ourselves in the joy of exploring without an agenda. Enjoy the colors and textures without any worries that there is a right way to do this. You may want to make several copies of the spiral to play with.

You will need:

Surfaces: A variety of flat textured surfaces. These can be anything from a plastic placemat, to corrugated cardboard, to the surface of your driveway. Look around in your kitchen or recycling bin to find interesting surfaces with bumps, dots, lines, pits, grates etc.

Crayons: Peel the paper off, as you will be using the sides of the crayon to rub.

A copy of the spiral page from the end of this chapter: You may download the image from the website or copy it from the book.

Lay the spiral page on top of a textured surface. Choose a colored crayon and rub it onto the paper applying enough pressure so that the texture below shows up on the paper. Play with as many colors and textures as you like while you cover the page, moving the various textures to different areas under the paper. You may want to stagger the colors and textures or layer them to create new effects. You may want to go outside to find new textured surfaces to rub.

Allow your self to relax and have fun. Let the spiral speak to you at a soul level. Take note of how you feel and any thoughts that arise. Reflect on the patterns that emerge in the colorful layers. Pay attention to any metaphors that present themselves. You will be activating your intuitive powers by focusing on the interplay of textures and colors rather than on words or exact images. Display the spirals or save them somewhere where you can refer to them often.

The symbol of the spiral will continue to speak to us as we move through each chapter of this book. Our understanding of our own creative nature evolves and changes like the budding rose that blooms, matures, falls away and buds again. We are just beginning to get the picture of this dynamic process and to see how our participation in the activities propels our understanding. As you make your way through the spiral metaphor you will be circling back around many times to find new perspectives on your creative nature.

Affirmation of Creativity

The final action for each chapter is writing an affirmation. These positive statements allow us to activate our imagination, creating a picture of how our lives look with that positive energy in it. This activity sets in motion the creative process of feeling and then, acting on that feeling.

Keep in mind that your affirmation does not need to be elaborate. Something as simple as "I am creative" will work great. Beginning your statement with "I am" or "I feel" invites your body, mind, heart and spirit to align. Then write out what it is that you would like to feel, have, create, or know as if it is already a reality. You are imagining what you want and enjoying the associated feelings in the present moment. In this way you focus your energy on those things, feelings and thoughts that bring you a sense of joy and accomplishment which fuels your actions and daily choices.

There are many great resources with affirmations that are ready to use, including Eric Maisel's book, *Affirmations for Artists*. I like Unity Church's *Daily Word*, which you can find online. The affirmations in these collections can be a great addition to the ones that you will write for yourself.

Read the affirmation presented. Notice how it feels to you. If the words hold meaning for you, create a way to display that affirmation, as well as the one that you create, so that you can read them often.

Where can you put the affirmation so that you can easily enjoy the lift that repeating it offers? You may want to write your affirmation out on a card to keep near your bed or at your desk so you can look at it before you start your day or your work. When you visit my house you will find affirmations printed out and stuck on my refrigerator, on my bathroom door and on the mirror in the hall way. Whenever I need to shift my energy I can easily read an affirming statement that redirects me. I choose to entertain the positive statements instead of any negative, limiting thoughts that are vying for attention.

AFFIRMATION

I Am Creative!

"I am a creative person who allows my sense of wonder and joy to open me up to new possibilities in my thoughts and actions. I claim my capacity for creating the positive changes in my life that will bring me into alignment with my vision of the life I want to live."

CREATE YOUR OWN AFFIRMATION

Now create your own affirmation of creativity. Begin with the word "I" and use words that describe how you want to feel and what you would like to experience. Engage your imagination as you write out a description of the ways that you see yourself living creatively.

Chapter Two

Spirited: Connecting to Our Individuality

"The true spiritual secret is this:
what you seek you already are.
True success is discovering your inner divinity.
It's the ability to love and have compassion,
trust your intuition, and awaken
your unlimited creative nature."

DEEPAK CHOPRA

Living a spirited, creative life requires us to be self-aware, to spiral inward to our center so that we are clear about who we are and how we want to be. As we honor our individual spirit and express our own uniqueness, we can more fully contribute our gifts and talents to the world.

We begin with our exploration into the center of the spiral, the place of our "unlimited creative nature." This is your individual spirit that we are talking about. Spirit — some would call it "soul" — in this sense is not meant in a specific religious way, but more as your essential self. You may prefer using the word "spark." Some may like the term "inner goddess," or "Source," or "Christ self." Go with what makes you most comfortable. You might also want to journal about the terms with which you are least comfortable to help you explore what about those terms disturbs you.

For some of you, the word "spirit" will include a connection with a spiritual source outside of yourself. This may be in the form of a specific god, a loving spirit or universal energy. Each of you will incorporate your own religious or spiritual practices into your creative life according to your own beliefs. The emphasis here will be on getting to know yourself in a deep and full way. This includes both your conscious self and those parts of your self that you are not conscious of.

In her book, *Conscious Money: Living, Creating, and Investing with Your Values for a Sustainable New Prosperity*, Patricia Aburdene says, "To be genuinely creative, you must nurture and readily access your personal connections to higher consciousness." You may interpret higher consciousness to mean that part in you which is connected to a source outside of yourself, or that which is in you that is the most fully conscious. This is yet another way of describing your spirit. When we bring our awareness to our strengths, our skills, our fears, and our life experiences we open our channels for making that connection with our higher selves.

Connecting with Our Attributes

"...Do you know what you are? You are a marvel.
You are unique. In all the years that have passed,
there has never been another child like you..."

PABLO PICASSO

Each of us truly is a marvel, a complex and wondrous being full of humanity and capable of amazing feats. We are mystical in our ability to create the life that we desire. Many different qualities contribute to our unique blend of individuality. We have a distinctive way that we interpret and translate our life experiences, approach our daily challenges, and relate to our fellow beings and to the world around us.

Has anyone ever asked you: What are your greatest strengths? This is a typical job interview question, which makes sense, because answering this question helps to clarify and paint the picture of the essence of who we are and how we connect with the world. This could also be framed as, "Tell us about your spirit." Identifying and magnifying those things about us that contribute the most to our expansive growth allows us to claim our power to create joyful success in our life. Claiming our strengths makes us stronger.

SHINE ON

Our Strengths and Our Tweaks

Imagine that you are going to be interviewed for the professional position of your dreams. Knowing that you will be asked to describe yourself and the unique strengths that you bring to the table, prepare a summary of your finest attributes. Write out all of the best qualities you have and how they assist you in solving problems. Give examples of how you have used your strengths, skills, talents, attitudes, and experiences in positive ways to impact your life and the lives of others. This is not just a list of things that you have done: it is a description of who you are.

For example, you might have a great sense of humor, or might be a forgiving friend. You may be very tenacious which gives you the staying power to finish a project. You may be a "big picture" person or, alternatively, you might

39

be one who is very detailed. Each of your attributes can make a contribution, so describe yourself in the most positive way possible.

Use this list to get you started:

1. Strengths

2. Skills

3. Talents

4. Attitudes

5. Experiences

Next, set up a pretend interview with yourself in front of a mirror, or use your computer to record yourself. Ask yourself: What are your strongest attributes?

Speak aloud what you have prepared. Do this several times until you can speak about yourself confidently, without hesitation. Journal about how it feels to claim your essential qualities.

Often times the question about our strengths is accompanied by the question: "What are your weaknesses?" This is also a revealing question and deserves some thought. See if you can diffuse any pejorative energy that the word "weak" holds for you. Frame this as an opportunity to look honestly at those things that you most likely would like to change. We can learn a great deal by shining a light on our weak links. You might like to use the word "tweak" instead of weak as it implies an action. I'll use the word "tweaks" in the Create to Relate activity that follows.

Ask yourself:

1. What do I most want to improve about myself?

2. Where do I see the need for growth?

3. What about myself do I perceive that I need to bring acceptance to?

4. What do I want to tweak or change?

Listen carefully. Allow time for the answers to work their way into a form that you can accept. Write about this in your journal along with your positive qualities and strengths. Try not to judge or criticize yourself. Being the compassionate observer of all that makes us who we are, gives us a chance to practice self-love and acceptance.

⌒

CREATE TO RELATE
Building on Your Strengths

"Once we believe in ourselves, we can risk curiosity, wonder, spontaneous delight, or any other experience that reveals the human spirit."

E. E. CUMMINGS

Did you ever make a paper chain? Perhaps you did when you were a child. Many of the activities in this book are designed to be very childlike in order to allow you to enter into this exploration with a childlike curiosity and wonder. Playing is fun but research shows that child's play is very important to the growth of children. I invite you to approach this activity with a playful heart.

This activity uses the technique for chain making in a new way. You will be working three-dimensionally to create a shape or structure as you explore your strengths and "tweaknesses."

You will need:
Paper: Strips of colorful construction paper about one inch wide and four inches long
Tape and colorful pens
Use your reflections on your strengths and your weaknesses (which I am now calling "tweaks") from the Shine On exercise that you just completed. Write each of your strengths on a separate strip of paper. Do the same for your tweaks. Make a loop with one of your strength strips and tape the ends together to form a loop. Take a strip with one of your tweaks on it and put it through the loop, then tape the end together. Continue to loop the strips so that every tweak is connected to at least two strengths. Play with this so that you are not making a linear chain. Watch as your creation takes shape and form.

What does the shape bring to mind? How do you use your strengths to overcome the challenges that your tweaks present? Do you see how your different attributes are all related? Reflect on the way that each part of you contributes to your whole self.

What Do You Value?

> *"You are what your deep driving desire*
> *is: as your deep driving desire is, so is*
> *your will, as your will is so is your deed,*
> *as is your deed so is your destiny."*
> THE UPANISHADS

Claiming our individual spirit includes identifying and clarifying what it is that is most important to us in our lives. That's why so many psychologists, coaches, counselors and spiritual leaders urge us to take the time to identify what we value. There are many tools available with lists of qualities that you can choose from, or you can generate a list of our own. One popular exercise is to read through an established list of qualities and circle everything that you value. Then narrow that list down to five qualities or to group them into strings that are similar.

Having a list to work from can be a good place to start, but generating your own ideas seems to be a very powerful way of coming closer to your true core. If you develop a habit of thinking about what your priorities are, it will give meaning to your daily choices. Being aware of what we value encourages us to be in the world in a way that is meaningful to us and aligns us with our individual spirit.

Take a look at the list of words that you wrote out in Chapter One when thinking about what creativity means to you. Now look at the Creativity Cards that you created with the ten to twelve most compelling words. How do these words relate to what is most important to you?

SHINE ON

Becoming Aware of What You Value

Use your Creativity Cards as a starting point to write about what it is that you hold dear. Read through your cards and pay close attention to how you feel about each concept. Ask yourself:

1. How is this important to me?

2. How does this motivate me?

3. What is missing?

4. What else do I value and why?

Take as long as you need with this activity. Add in any concepts that you value that were not on your Creativity cards. Listen carefully to your body's sensations, your thoughts, and your feelings, as they will help you to clarify the importance of each concept. There is no need to cull through and reduce this down to a single value or set of values.

Be present to knowing clearly what you find deeply meaningful, what you want to incorporate into your daily life, and what gives you a reason for being. Notice how these intertwine, overlap and weave together. Some of these values will hold true for you throughout your life. It's also possible that things will shift in importance. Can you think of a time when something in your life changed and you found that what you valued changed as well?

You will return to this work with what you value when you get to Chapter Six.

CREATE TO RELATE

House of Values

Have you ever made a house of cards? This was a popular rainy day activity way back before the advent of video games. All it took was a deck of cards and some patient determination.

Using the cards you made with your power creativity words, build a structure of your own design. Begin by leaning two cards with your most cherished concepts against each other on a flat surface —like a table with a cloth on it, or the carpeted floor—until they can stand on their own. Add in other cards by leaning them gently against the two beginning cards, to create a base. Carefully extend the structure outward and upward. Notice what takes place. Write about your experience.

1. What happened with your house of cards?

2. What connections come to mind for you?

3. What is it that combines with your values to complete the structure of your spirited life?

Let these questions float around inside your body and mind for a while before attempting to make sense of them.

Ways of Being

"Our individuality is all, all that we have.
There are those who would barter it for
security, but blessed in the twinkle of the
Morningstar is the one who nurtures and
rides it, in grace and love and wit."
TOM ROBBINS

Defining our individual spirit is an organic process that circles us around our full range of emotions, our strengths, our challenges, and what we value in our life. We are shining a light on every aspect of who we are, including both those parts that are easily known and those that are mostly hidden but that are parts of our essential selves. In our efforts to get a clear picture of who we are, we can look at a couple of other factors that influence how we are in the world. These include our style of learning, and our energy around interacting with others.

I remember sitting in a psychology class at the University of San Diego (Go Toreros!) and hearing that people have different learning styles. Some people are visual learners while others are auditory, or kinesthetic learners. I considered myself smart and I had always been an academically high achiever. However, in order to digest the material in my college level psychology classes, I had taken to reading out loud to myself as I walked up and down the aisles of an empty classroom at night. I tried so hard to absorb the meaning from the page by just reading it, but I was always falling asleep.

When I realized that I had an auditory and kinesthetic learning style it was as if Major-League-Baseball field-at-night type lights came on! The way that I found I could really make a connection with the material was if I heard it. Better yet, I found that if I could physically act it out or move to the information in some meaningful way, I was able to truly understand it and retain what I had learned. I had discovered my best way to learn and I knew that I would have to make adaptations that suited me if I was going to succeed in a university environment.

Howard Gardner's work on multiple intelligences broadened our understanding of the many diverse ways that people interact with and process information and the world around them. Here are a few of the different ways that people lean or how we can be "smart."

Linguistic	Word smart
Logical	Mathematical/reasoning smart
Visual Spatial	Picture smart
Auditory	Sound smart
Kinesthetic	Body smart
Musical	Music smart
Interpersonal	People smart

Intrapersonal	Self smart
Naturalist	Nature smart
Urban	Survival Street smart
Spiritual	Spiritually smart

Many of us have found ourselves in situations that emphasized a type of processing that was not our primary learning style. Traditional education models have not always recognized and utilized the full range of possible intelligences. But once we are clear on how we interact with information and can identify our primary style, we can make choices that highlight our innate abilities and support our success. There are many different ways of being successful. Knowing your personal style centers you in your individual spirit.

SHINE ON

Identifying Your Learning Style

Focus on the ways that you learn best. Write about your learning style using the following prompts.

1. In what ways do I learn best?

2. What different kinds of "smart" describe the way that I interact with the world?

3. How does that affect the choices that I make in my work? Home life? What about in my relationships?

4. Do I have any other kinds of "smarts" other than the ones listed above?

5. In what ways do I want to process all that I am discovering while on the path of the spiral of creativity?

The Shine On activities are awareness activities based on writing but writing is just a suggestion. The Create to Relate activities offer opportunities for you to use a variety of modalities to interact with the material in this book. Feel free to find your own way of expressing your unique style. You are encouraged to invent ways to explore creativity that fit your learning style. Are you a kinesthetic learner? Then by all means add movement into any of the suggested activities. Musical? Create a song or use an instrument.

Here are a few more fun ideas for expanding your creative experience while you play with different modalities:

- Sounds: Whisper, shout, sing, hum, tap it out, strum, play it on an instrument

- Visuals: Paint, stitch, weave, carve, stamp, cut, collage, photograph

- Movement: Twirl, glide, leap, skip, slide, tilt, bend, twist

- Language: Poems, stories, articles,

- Tempo: Fast, slow, staccato, heavy, light like a….

You can fill in your ideas for any or all of the "smarts" listed in the section above. Use this as a springboard for creating your own resource for creative expression. There is no right or wrong way so have fun and personalize the activities as you go.

Interaction and Energy

*"You need Chaos in your soul to
give birth to a dancing star."*
FRIEDRICH NIETZCHE

Years after college when my children were very young,
I made another life-changing discovery. A friend recom-
mended a book that I still use and value today: *Raising
Your Spirited Child: A Guide for Parents Whose Child is More
Intense, Sensitive, Perceptive, Persistent and Energetic* by Mary
Sheedy Kurcinka. In this book, the author encourages us
to bring our awareness to the differences between people
who are introverted and people who are extroverted. The
key is in the way that they find and maintain their energy.
This perspective changed my way of interacting with my
husband and children and gave me insights into my own
way of being in the world.

According to Kurcinka, the terms "extrovert" and "intro-
vert" refer to the different ways people get and store their
energy for day-to-day living. This concept is based on the-
ories of psychological types described by Carl Jung, and
suggests that the way we fuel ourselves is a predetermined
part of who we are. Knowing how we get energized is an
important part of our self-knowledge and can help us to
choose ways of being that support us best.

According to Jung, introverts prefer time alone to
recharge. They find extended interaction with others requires
high amounts of their energy so being in groups for too long
really drains them. They also like to have personal space that
protects them from overusing their energy. Introverts are
more likely to do their thinking before they speak and will
take time to reflect before offering an opinion.

Extroverts recharge by interacting with others. They love to talk things out, problem-solve out loud, and exchange ideas. These are the "people" people. Any chance to interact with others gives them a chance to refuel. Social situations are where they thrive, while too much time alone robs them of their energetic edge. Traditionally, extroverts have been the ones in leadership roles and positions of power.

Lately, there has been a new awareness about the role that introverts play in contributing to our culture. Susan Cain, in her book *Quiet: The Power of Introverts in a World that Can't Stop Talking* brings awareness to the qualities of introverted people that lead to innovation and creative breakthroughs. The more that we, as a society, learn about the different ways that people interact in our world, the better we can apply this awareness to education, business and personal development. Your personal awareness of your way of being in the world is essential to mastering your spirited life.

SHINE ON

Clarifying Your Energy Style

Shine a light on how you get and maintain your energy and how that affects your work, your home life, your relationships and your creative choices. Use the following questions as prompts to write about your energy style.

1. What do I do to energize myself for my creative work?

2. At the end of the day, how do I like to regain my energy?

3. How do I see my relationships with others in terms of energy output and input?

4. What is my ideal work situation?

5. What activities require the most energy? How do I ensure that I am up for it?

6. What does it feel like to be full of energy? Physically? Emotionally?

7. What do I feel like when I'm running low on energy? Physically? Emotionally?

8. What can I do to keep my flow of energy?

Once you become very clear about the way that you learn and the way that you interact and use your energy, you are on your way to being able to apply that knowledge to your relationships and your work. Your style is important and does not have to be the same style as those you interact with. Knowing that there are many different ways of being in this world and respecting that we each have our own way of learning and refueling, helps us to understand and empathize with ourselves and each other.

This chapter has focused our attention on some of the factors that are essential to our "individual-ness." I like to encourage my clients to claim their "ness" as I might claim my "Brecia-ness." When we are acting from our "ness," or essential self, there is a sense of truly being centered and a feeling of authentic joy. We will extend our exploration of individual spirit when we get to Chapter Six and focus on our authenticity. Remember, this is not a linear process!

CREATE TO RELATE

Creating a Spirit Circle

You have been focusing your awareness on your individual spirit in your Shine On writing exercises, which primarily utilize your language-centered thinking. You have been encouraged to connect your thoughts with how you feel both emotionally and physically. You have also practiced using different modalities while doing the Create to Relate activities. Now, you will once again shift into employing your non-language-oriented faculties. The idea is to use as many different ways to perceive yourself as possible.

To create your Spirit Circle, you will use photos and pictures as a tool for communicating with your inner wisdom. By paying close attention to your physical and emotional reaction to the images, you bypass your intellect and let your feelings help you to open up to that which is not consciously known to you. By working with a circular shape you reinforce that your creative journey is not a linear process but is more cyclical.

You will need:

Old magazines

Paper

Glue

Scissors

Use old magazines to collect images as you focus on your strengths, your values, and your learning and energy styles. Let your mind wander while you scan the images and choose those that you react to either physically or emotionally. Cut them out. Do not use words.

Draw a large circle on a piece of paper and cut it out. Arrange the images on the circle in a way that feels right to you. Don't try to organize them with your left-brain thinking. Just let the images guide you. When you are done arranging, glue them down. Let this collage dry and hang it in a place where you will see it every day. Notice any messages or connections that you become aware of. You may be surprised as you work your way through this book, how this activity may support your self-discovery.

SPIRAL ACTIVITY

A Spirit Mandala

Here is another way for us to connect with our inner spirit. This time we will be combining words, pattern and colors. Using the symbol of the mandala as an inspiration, we will be creating a design to help us focus on the unity of our individual spirit. "Mandala" is a Sanskrit word for "circle." The mandala has been used in Hindu, Buddhist and Tibetan cultures as a spiritual tool for cultivating awareness.

You will need:

A spiral page from the end of the chapter: You may want to make copies of the spiral so that you can work with them out of the book.

Color-makers: Crayons, watercolor paints, chalk pastels, colored pencils, etc. Lighter applications of colors will work best so that you can see the writing beneath the color.

Using dark markers on the large spiral page at the end of this chapter, write your valued qualities along the spiral, placing those things that you value most, closest to the center. Add in your strengths, your "tweaknesses," your learning style, your energy style and anything else that feels important to your individual spirit. Write them into the spiral so that they fill the spaces throughout the spiral shape.

Circle or highlight the words in some way, then create a pattern by connecting them with curved or straight lines. Using the full spectrum of the rainbow, apply a light layer of paint or color to the spiral using gold at the center and then proceeding outward to orange, red, purple, blue and green. You can create a pattern that is as simple or complex as you want. Take your time. Honor the beautiful spirit that you are with vibrant color.

The Spirit Mandala that you have created is a colorful representation of your individual spirit. Seeing the colors and patterns allows you a new way of seeing your individuality and a way for your deeper self to express itself. You may want to do this activity again as you work your way through this book. Notice any changes or new revelations as you repeat this exercise.

AFFIRMATION

I Am Spirited

"As a creative person I am called to infuse my work with spirit, to bring it to life. I breathe a little bit of my soul into everything I create. I am ardent, energetic, and vivacious as I courageously explore new ideas, techniques, and avenues of expression using my unique talents and style. I bring my awareness to what I value most in life and make choices accordingly."

CREATE YOUR OWN SPIRITED AFFIRMATION

You may want to refer back to Chapter One to review how to write an affirmation. Remember to begin with an "I" statement and engage your imagination with expressive action words.

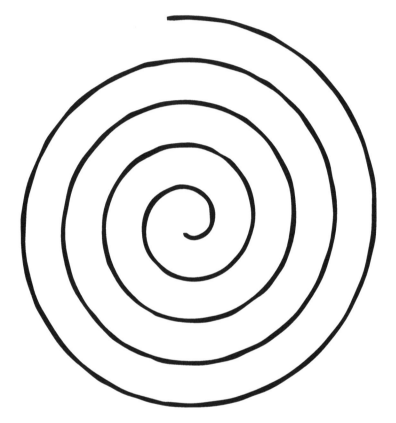

Chapter Three

Passionate:
Fueling Our Creativity

"Passion is something within you that
provides the continual enthusiasm, focus
and energy you need to succeed."

JACK CANFIELD

Passion fuels our creativity by igniting our hearts, spirits, minds and bodies so that we have the full use of our whole selves to create. It energizes us by urging us to focus in on what we feel compelled to be, do, or have and it supplies us with the motivation to meet the challenges and obstacles that may get in our way. Being passionate about something drives us toward it. Excitement may run high when we are feeling our passion, or it may work like a laser to concentrate our energy in one direction.

Not only can our passion propel us toward a singular goal, our feelings of love actually create a store of energy that we can apply in whatever direction that we want. By kindling our passion for one thing, we are uplifted and fueled across the board as well. It is like filling your gas tank or as Julia Cameron puts it, "filling the well."

We can stir our passions by taking time to pay attention to what we really love and to notice what makes us happy, fills us with joy, makes us tingle, and gets us all goose-bumpy. The alignment that takes place when we feel passionate changes our whole being. Picture a slot machine with body, mind, heart, and spirit all lined up, lights flashing, sirens blaring, and the big payout flashing across the screen.

Some of us are jump-up-and-down-and-clap-our-hands kind of people. We react to things in a physical and obvious way. It's easy for us to identify the things that really stir us, the things that we love. Perhaps you are not prone to goose bumps. You may feel your passion in a more subtle way. How we experience the stirrings in our hearts is as individual as we are. Here is where our different ways of being may come into play. For some, identifying the things that we love may be very easy. For others it may take some time to tune in to our heart and open up the space for passion to rise up and be recognized. But our passion will be felt in a real and physical way.

How does your passion fuel you? Shining a light on the things that we love is like putting a log onto the fire. When we pay close attention to our physical sensation of love and use our senses as a guide, we center our passionate energy in our bodies. Keeping a list of the things that you love to see, hear, feel, taste, do or make is like having energy bars with you when you hike. You can refuel by referring to your list and incorporating those things into your daily life. Pay close attention to your body sensations, your emotional responses, and your thoughts when you are engaged in your creative work and you will learn to apply the fuel that you gain from engaging in your passionate activities to every situation.

You may have the idea that to "follow your bliss" means that if you pursue something you are passionate about as your life's work, then, you will be happy. I'm proposing that you start by engaging in all of the different things that you love and that make you happy, and then any work that you do will be fueled by that passionate energy. I'd also suggest that fueling your love center is important for your own self-acceptance and for sharing compassion with others.

✁

SHINE ON

Passion as Fuel

*"What you love is a sign from your
higher self of what you are to do."*

Sanya Roman

How do you know that you are engaged in something that you are passionate about? How does that feel? Do you find that you are thinking about the activity all of the time? When you are engaged in the activity do you lose track of time? Would you do this for free or even pay to do it? Write out all of the details of how your passions affect you mentally and emotionally.

Now let's add in our physical and sensual experience. Using all of your senses take a moment to imagine each sight, sound, smell, touch and feel that you love. Use the prompts below to write out twelve things that you feel passionate about. Add all of the details needed to create a vibrant picture of your passions.

1. I am passionately thrilled when I see...

2. I am passionately thrilled when I see...

3. I am passionately thrilled when I hear...

4. I am passionately thrilled when I hear...

5. I am passionately thrilled when I feel...

6. I am passionately thrilled when I feel...

7. I am passionately thrilled when I taste...

8. I am passionately thrilled when I taste...

9. I am passionately thrilled when I smell...

10. I am passionately thrilled when I smell...

11. I am passionately thrilled when I do...

12. I am passionately thrilled when I make...

Here are a few other phrases you might choose to use as prompts:

1. I love to....

2. I'm crazy about....

3. ...tickles me pink!

4. I feel fabulous when I....

5. I could...all day long.

You get the idea. Play with the different phrases to see what comes to mind with each. When you are done writing, read over your list and descriptions. Pay attention to how your body feels as you think about what you love. Does thinking about what is on your list bring a smile to your face? Does it make you feel lighter, more energized and alive?

Clarifying what you are passionate about is the first step. Next, you become aware of how you experience that passionate energy in your body. Then, you can incorporate more of what you love into your daily life choices. Finally, you apply that energy to accepting yourself, expressing your creativity, and directing compassion toward others.

CREATE TO RELATE
Favorite Things

"Raindrops on roses and whiskers on kittens...." These song lyrics by Rogers and Hammerstein, are from the classic movie, *The Sound of Music.* The song is a list of things that the character Maria loves. She is singing about her favorite things because she is afraid, and thinking about what she loves gives her strength. Look at your list of things that you are passionate about. Another way of figuring out what you are passionate about is to list your favorite things.

Create a song using your list of favorite things. You might like to borrow the tune of the classic song or you can start from scratch with a new tune. You can try rhyming, rapping or chanting. Find your own way to bring voice to the things that you love. Have fun, and when you are done, share this with someone you love.

You may want to spiral back to this song once you have explored the rest of this chapter. Singing about what makes you happy can be a wonderful way to shift your energy when you find yourself challenged by self-doubt or fear.

If you are not a musical kind of person, you can jump in and give it a try, or you might like to create something different with your list of favorite things. Paint a picture, create a collage, cook an eight-course dinner, or choreograph a bit of a movement series. What other ways can you think of to express and celebrate your favorite things?

Self-Awareness and Self-Acceptance

*"Creativity is the ability to go from one failure
to another with no loss of enthusiasm."*
WINSTON CHURCHILL

Following our bliss and living fueled by our passion, is something that most of us creative folks aspire to. And yet, we so often find ourselves struggling to allow that to happen for ourselves. Although there may be many obstacles that present themselves while we are striving to master our spirited creative life, we often find that the most difficult obstacles are the ones that we experience internally. These are the thoughts and feelings that keep us small. They prevent us from expanding into our visions of what we want to be or to accomplish. Sheryl Sandberg, the Chief Operating Officer of Facebook, and author of *Lean In* says, "The role of internal obstacles is rarely discussed and often underplayed."

First, we are going to focus on the role our thoughts play as we strive to be creatively self-aware and centered in love. Two things that commonly get in our way are:

1. Long held stories or myths that we have adopted that limit our potential, and

2. Listening to our own critical voice when it does not support or nurture us.

Let's take a look at each of these.

Minimizing myths are the stories that we have told our selves, or have learned from others, that keep us from reaching beyond our comfort zone to the place where we will actually grow into our potential. Everyone loves a good story. We hold onto the story of how we can't do something or believe that we haven't got the right kind of (fill in the blank) to succeed. These "limiting beliefs" are thoughts that we hold to be true that are more opinion than fact. They are stories that have gone beyond their original life as an excuse and have taken on a mythic proportion. We mistake them for truth, but they are not true.

Even though a belief may have no validity, it still has the power to diminish our ability to love ourselves and to activate our love center for others. Minimizing myths may come from outside our selves, perhaps from a parent, a teacher, our boss or pop culture. They can also be something that we generated ourselves out of fear or pessimism. When we examine these stories and allow ourselves to see through them, we can then reclaim that power for ourselves.

Here are a few commonly held minimizing myths:

- I'm too old and it's too late to begin being creative.

- I don't have any talent.

- I'm just a mom and I don't have anything to offer.

The insidious thing about minimizing myths is that we have framed them as truths. We are not seeing them as thoughts of criticism, judgment, or self-degradation. It's possible that believing the myth allows us to stay in our comfort zone. Simply reframing the story, by turning it around and stating "I'm *not* too old," or "I *do* have talent" might be terrifying. Recognizing and acknowledging our fear of expanding into the unknown gives us the opportunity to experience courage. Our courage and our self-love go hand in hand.

What's Your Story?

What stories have you held on to that limit your sense of self and your creativity? Spiritual thought leader Byron Katie, in her work encourages us to challenge each of our stories or beliefs by asking ourselves: "Is that true?" This is one way of opening ourselves up to letting go of our myths.

Write out any minimizing myths that you think might be holding you back from fully engaging in your passionate, creative life. For each one, ask yourself: "Does this feel true for me now?"

Pay close attention to how your body responds. If you can answer "No," dispel that myth by writing out a new story statement to take its place. Connect with your courageous heart. Acknowledge the fear that you feel as well as your desire to move ahead, in spite of your fear. If the myth still feels real, write about what you would do differently if you did not believe the myth. You are the storyteller. You get to live the story that you choose.

What other ways can you make this new story come alive? What kinds of visuals would you create to accompany your story? What kind of soundtrack? Any dance numbers?

Learning to let go of our self-criticism is essential to our creative journey. After we become aware of our minimizing myths, we may still have internal language that inhibits us from moving fully into our new story. Eric Maisel, the author of *Coaching the Artist Within: Advice for Writers, Actors, Visual Artists, and Musicians from America's Foremost Creativity Coach* outlines ways for us to get a grip on our inner dialogue. He says that just really noticing what you say to yourself can make a world of difference. He suggests bringing our awareness to our negative inner thoughts, challenging them, and then replacing them with new, more empowering thoughts.

Many years ago, I read about psychiatrist Daniel Amen's suggestion that we turn our Automatic Negative Thoughts, ANTs, into Positive Energizing Thoughts, PETs. I love the image that this model conjures up and I find myself referencing the ANTs in my journal, usually marching "two by two, hurrah, hurrah!" When we pair the image of the ants, like the ones that come streaming up onto our porch after it rains, with our automatic thoughts, we get a picture of the tremendous power that we can harness by turning our thoughts into positive and energizing statements. Paying attention to our self-talk is an important step in helping us to center ourselves in love and acceptance.

There are certain circumstances in which our minimizing thoughts inevitably pop up. Anytime that we attempt something new or something that we don't feel confident about, or something that has challenged us in the past, we find that there are a whole set of thoughts that come up habitually. In order to break the habit of allowing them to affect us emotionally we shine a light on those thoughts, acknowledge them, accept them and exchange them for different, more empowering thoughts.

Affirmations

*"The mind is everything; what
you think, you become."*

BUDDHA

Our thoughts are energy and everything that exists in the world began with a thought. Whether you turn to physics, psychology, religion, or popular business strategy, you will see that people are using the principles of positive thinking to manifest the results they want in their lives. Volumes have been written about the power of visualization, imagining something as a way of experiencing it internally in order to anchor it in our external lives. Affirmations work in the same way as visualizations.

Affirmations are positive statements that bring us the feeling of expansion and align us with our passionate energy. Using them gives us a "sense of safety and hope" according to Julia Cameron, the author of *The Artist's Way*. Even when we are not feeling our positive energy flowing, stating a feeling of joy, love, peace, or prosperity gives us the opportunity to kick-start a new perspective. We try on the positive words, let them inspire a shift, and open ourselves up to a new way of being. This is why we have been including affirmations in each chapter of *The Spiral of Creativity*.

SHINE ON

The Power of Affirmations

While listening to your internal talk, take note of any criticisms, judgments, or minimizing thoughts that make you feel contracted, belittled and ineffective. Go to your love center and simply observe these thoughts without adding any emotional energy to them.

Fold a piece of paper in half. On one side of the paper, write out any self-doubts, criticisms or judgments that come up for you. On the other side write out three affirming statements that convert the energy of each negative statement. Read the affirming statements out loud several times.

For example: If you have written a self-criticism like: "I always mess up when I'm trying to explain to people what it is that I do. I'm so dumb!" You can shift the negative energy of that thought with these positive and true statements:

"I'm able to share what I do with people in a way that is easy for them to understand and that allows me to express my joy at being of service."

"I'm a capable communicator."

"I'm willing to accept that I sometimes goof up, but I know that I can share my gifts with others because I am an intelligent person with real skills to offer."

Do you recognize the difference in the energy present in these statements? Why not claim the more positive thoughts as the ones that you want to practice and choose not to give power to the negative thoughts that do not support you? Your ability to accept and love yourself begins with your own internal dialogue.

If you'd like, hold your paper as if you were a town crier, making a pronouncement from the Queen or King. Ham it up! Play with it. Begin with, "Hear ye! Hear ye!" From this moment forward, in the land of..., I do proclaim...."

Decorate your declaration or put it to music. Use your most comfortable way of expressing yourself or challenge yourself to use the way you are least comfortable with.

CREATE TO RELATE

Affirmation Cards

So far, you have played with making Spiral Cards and Creativity Word Cards. Here is another way to make a set of cards to use to support your ability to center yourself in love. Cards are small and portable and they work for us the way a coach or guide would. They can be used to remind us of important truths that we sometimes let slip below our radar. These cards will be particularly powerful as they reinforce the loving energy that is specifically designed to meet your own personal challenges.

You will need:
Card stock or heavy paper
Acrylic paints
Brushes
Sponges
Stamps

Using acrylic paints, go wild and have fun turning the paper into a wonderland of color and texture. You can use a brush or for more fun just finger paint. You may want to decorate your paper with spirals. No need to worry about this being judged. After the color dries, cut the paper into cards and write one of your new positive, energizing affirmations on each card. You can make a card for each of the affirmations that you write at the end of each chapter as well.

Feel free to decorate these cards using any other art materials that you like. You can make a collage of pictures from magazines, or use colored pencils, stamps or stencils. Cut them into a variety of shapes or keep them uniform.

I recommend that you keep these cards near your bed so you can read them in the morning as you start your day or put them on the desk where you work so you can read them throughout the day. I like to keep some affirmation cards in my car. I also have them hanging from a branch suspended in front of the entrance to my art studio so that everyone who enters into the space passes below the positive statements. Affirming, positive energy thoughts nourish your passion center and keep you enthusiastic and focused.

Compassion and Fear

*"I will not die an unlived life. I will not live in
fear of falling or catching fire. I choose to inhabit
my days, to allow my living to open me, to make
me less afraid, more accessible, to loosen my heart
until it becomes a wing, a torch, a promise. I choose
to risk my significance to live so that which came
to me as blossom, goes on as fruit."*

DAWNA MARKOVA

Bringing our awareness to our passions and to our capacity for love, we have found that we may also encounter our feelings of anxiety, fear, and doubt. Even when we address our limiting thoughts, we still have an emotional component that we need to shine a light on. When we open the door to love, those other feelings come rushing through as well.

The trick is to recognize all of our feelings so that we can experience what it is that they have to teach us. By inviting our fear and doubt to come forward right there with our passionate love feelings we have the opportunity to experience them in a way that doesn't deplete our energy. Since fear is really the opposite of love, our challenge is to be fueled by love without letting our fear stand in the way of our creating the lives we desire for ourselves.

How can we embrace both our passion and our fear so that we feel free to create? We can learn to become aware of our fears, to accept our fears as a part of who we are, and to treat ourselves with compassion. We can balance our choices by embracing the things that we love and recognizing that we can be gentle and kind when dealing with our fears.

Taking a good look at our fears and getting familiar with them will help us to know how much we need to pay attention to what each fear has to teach us. Fear may appear if your new creative adventure is skydiving out of airplanes, but it also may appear when you want to take a drawing class. In the first case, you want to pay close attention to this fear and allow it to provide you with the necessary caution to proceed. In the second case, recognizing this fear, accepting that it is a part of you and then moving past it will allow you to explore and invest your energy in a new, but not intrinsically dangerous, creative activity.

Perhaps you fear that being creative means that you will not be safe. You fear that giving into your creative side will lead you into dangerous situations. There may be a good reason why you harbor this fear. Perhaps you knew someone who took a creative risk that ended badly. Fearing for our safety is not only natural it is essential for our survival. As you enter into a new creative venture this fear may arise because you are entering into the unknown. How can we learn to pay attention to our fears without letting them overwhelm us?

What can we do to develop a familiarity with our fears? Journaling about how we feel can be extremely helpful. As you journal, you may find that you have themes of reoccurring thoughts of fear or self-doubt that appear in your writing. After awhile, you will be able to recognize the usual suspects that show up like a casting call. Thoughts like these may circle around, and come back often, even after we feel that we have faced them, accepted them, and put them aside. For example:

"I feel like a fake."

"Nothing I do has any meaning or value."

"I'm afraid of looking dumb, of not being enough, of not being taken seriously."

When we are able to see these feelings as a normal part of our creative angst, we can observe them without experiencing the emotional impact that they originally carried. We have seen them before, perhaps many times. They even may have once played an important part in our growth process by slowing us down and forcing us to question our actions. We may find that they pop up automatically in times of stress. They are still useful because they provide a check in for us. Each time these fearful thoughts and feelings appear, we have the opportunity to practice self-love and acceptance. We can use affirmations as a tool to help us shift into the love zone.

✂

SHINE ON

Your Usual Suspects

Find a comfortable place to write that feels safe and private. Light a candle or some incense to create a feeling of peace and openness. Bring an image of something you love and set it in front of you. Focus on your breathing, inhaling fully and exhaling slowly. Gently roll your head from side to side. Bring your shoulders up near your ears and drop them to release tensions that appear. When you are ready, allow your mind to adopt an attitude of curiosity. Open your journal and begin a dialog with your fear.

What thoughts of fear or self-doubt do you find recurring in your mind over and over again? Who are your usual suspects? Can you name each fear? Invite your fears to tell you all about themselves. Ask each one why it is there and what it has to teach you. Listen carefully. Write down your conversation. Your soul may want to contribute to this exploration in ways other than through words. Sketch, or draw, or doodle as well as you listen. Be aware of any images that float up into your mind. Note any bodily sensations that feel relevant. Continue to be the curious observer.

You are in charge. Take this slowly, so that you don't get overwhelmed. You may want to limit your exploration to just one fear at a time. When you are done interviewing your fear, thank it for sharing with you and tell it that you accept it as one of your feelings. Notice the connection that your fear has to love. Affirm your feelings of self-love as you finish your writing session. You can use the affirmations that you have written or you can simply say, "Love. Love. Love." I like to add, "Right here, right now."

When a fearful thought comes into your mind, it also registers in your body. We may feel a tensing in our gut or shoulders. Our bodies may ache or shake. Our breathing may quicken, or we may find it hard to catch our breath. We may feel our hearts beat in our chests. We may feel clammy or sweaty.

Noticing all of your physical reactions to fearful thoughts gives you the chance to address these feelings within your body. Practicing a few simple techniques for relaxing and expanding may counter the contraction that your fear causes. Here are some suggestions for releasing the tension that accompanies our feelings of fear.

1. Take slow deep breaths. Focus on your inhale, filling your lungs completely. Then exhale consciously allowing your muscles to relax as you do.

2. Roll and shrug our shoulders to release the tension. Consciously allow your gut to relax.

3. Calm yourself by allowing yourself to compassionately recognize your fear as a part of who you are. Offer your fear acceptance and thank it for the part it plays in keeping you safe.

4. Tell your fear that although you recognize it is real and a part of you, you choose to allow yourself to continue to expand with love, even as you enter into the unknown.

5. Engage in one of the activities that you love to do.

6. Use your senses. Smells can be very calming. Look for a touch of beauty in your immediate environment. Listen for bird song or the sound of children playing or turn on your favorite music. Close your eyes and feel the sunshine on your skin or feel the crisp cool air, or brisk breeze. Tune into the sensations on your skin as you release any tension you are feeling.

7. Water soothes. Whether you sink into a spa, or bathtub or simple rinse your hands under the faucet, water has a nourishing effect. Don't forget to drink it as well.

8. Allow the symbol of the spiral to remind you that you are on a journey and that you will pass through all of your feelings on your way. Choose to feel love even as you allow yourself to feel fear.

CREATE TO RELATE

Create a Sanctuary for Your Fear

Here is an opportunity to bring a playful energy to familiarizing your most frequently felt fears. You will be creating a sanctuary for your feelings, a physical place where you can interact with all of your emotions in a safe way. By bringing your imagination and creativity to this exercise, you can diffuse some of the power that these fears have to limit you. Let your childlike curiosity replace judgment as you observe these parts of yourself that can be challenging.

Center yourself in love. Use an affirmation or a love mantra. You may want to light some incense or play your favorite music. Use your favorite colors while you create and delight in the creative ideas that come to you as you create this sanctuary for your feelings.

You will need:
A large piece of cardboard
Paints and color makers
Old magazines
Scissors
Glue

On a large piece of cardboard, create a park-like setting which can become a preserve where your fears can wander around but are still confined. Think of it as a wild animal sanctuary. Use old boxes, plastic containers, paper, or other goodies from your recycling bin, as well as some paints to create your park. Include a variety of environmental elements like large, open spaces, watering holes, hills, valleys, caves, or perches. Make some kind of border to assure that the sanctuary is contained.

Take an inventory of your fears and write out a name for each one that you can identify. Create an image or object that seems to fit each fear. You may want to draw or paint, cut out pictures from magazines or assign found objects to them. Place your fears into the sanctuary. Imagine that this place of feelings is like a safety zone a little bit like a wild animal reserve. You can observe and interact with your challenging feelings while they are safely in the sanctuary so that you can confidently handle them when they appear as you explore the creative unknown. Most importantly, you will have a chance to love and accept each part of who you are.

The Story of the Biting Fish

One night I had this dream:

I was walking down a welcomingly worn dirt path through a thickly wooded canyon. A creek bubbled along near the path, the sunlight danced on the water and dappled the leaves, and the air felt wonderfully cool on my skin. I smiled with a sense of ease, knowing I was on my right path. I felt blessed and happy. All was well.

Then out of the corner of my eye, I saw something jumping in the creek water very nearby. It was a fish and it was snapping its mouth full of teeth at me. Then another, and another snapping fish jumped into the air. I was really unnerved. I started to flee down the path. Now I was on my bicycle but the fish pursued me, snapping at my heels and ankles. I tried to kick them away, but they were persistent. I was getting upset. I was incredulous that this could be happening to me when I had been so very happy to be here, just a moment before.

I awoke wondering what that was all about. Then I remembered that the day before, I had given a presentation. Everything had gone smoothly. The talk was well received and many people commented how much they enjoyed what I had to share. I was quite pleased at first, but soon began to berate myself with the many things that I should have done better. I should have done this or that differently; I should have done more; I should have left out this. On and on I went, barraging myself with "shoulds." The fear that I wasn't good enough overtook all of my feelings of happiness and accomplishment.

In my dream, I was happily moving along my right path, feeling content and grateful until the biting fish appeared. I had recreated the "shoulds" as annoying little piranhas, chasing after me and changing my experience of joy into one of fear and failure.

The next day, I was in a local gift shop and saw a bin of colorful, funny-looking, rubber fish. They had big bugged-out eyes and a goofy looks on their faces. I bought one in each color and brought them home. I put them into a small, round glass bowl and set them on the shelf in my studio. Seeing these silly fish in their bowl makes me smile. I let go of my tension, and breathe. This dissipates the fear and allows me to check in and ask myself: Is there something more to be learned from the appearance of the biting fish?

Creating a physical representation of my self-doubts helps me to accept these thoughts and feelings as a natural part of my creative process. This changes their energy and opens me up to hearing any messages that they have for me. Rather than feeling like a failure, I can curiously wonder if there were things that I might do differently next time to grow as a presenter. I can listen to the thoughts that arise, sort through them, and give weight to any that may help me to grow. Like our fears, these doubts foster the kinds of thoughts that we experience as contraction rather than expansion.

CREATE TO RELATE

Working with Your Sanctuary

Revisit the sanctuary that you built for your fears. Create a physical representation for your "shoulds" and place them in the sanctuary. You may want to create a special area for these kinds of thoughts. You can borrow my fish idea and make a pool of "shoulds" where you can easily interact with the ideas that limit your feelings of success. You can get familiar with your "shoulds" in the same way that you can observe your fears.

Make some popcorn and spend some time taking a tour of your "sanctuary." Imagine what your fears and shoulds are doing, how they interact, and also what they need. Speak lovingly to your fears and shoulds. Bring some humor into your conversation with them. You can tell them to "Chill out" or "Hang loose." You can share your creative dreams with them and let them know that they will not be in control. See what you can come up with to create an atmosphere of acceptance that feels right to you. Choose expansion beyond the limits that your fears and doubts allow.

Working from Our Passionate Center

"And as we let our own light shine, we unconsciously give other people permission to do the same. As we are liberated from our own fear, our presence automatically liberates others."
MARIANNE WILLIAMSON

Our passion fuels our creative life. The heart is commonly considered the center of passion. We relate matters of the heart to our emotions, our motivations, and our values. We apply our enthusiasm, focus, and energy to the things that call to us and in turn, they fuel us with more energy, focus and enthusiasm. The rhythm of our spiraling inward and outward mimics the pumping of our actual heart. Whether we look at the functioning of our physical body or the way that we express our individual spirit in the world, clearly our heart centers us and plays a crucial role in our growth.

SHINE ON

Working from Your Passionate Center

What does it mean to work from our passionate center, to put your heart into what you are creating? To create art that is a heartfelt response to something?

Working with heart might mean that you are creating for someone you love, something for your grandchild, your significant other or for a child or parent. Or it may involve creating work to donate to help others. Sometimes we use our creations to express the anger, frustration and indignation that we feel in our hearts.

Using the questions above and below, write about how your heart is connected to what you create.

1. What is in my heart that I would like to express?

2. How does my work connect me to those I love?

3. How does my heart connect with other creators?

4. How does my work connect me to strangers in need?

5. How can my work connect me to future generations?

Some of what you write here will help you to focus in on why you want to create. You will want to review this when you get to Chapter Six and begin to claim your inner authority. You may also want to look at the Shine On writing that you did in Chapter Two, when you were clarifying what you value.

SPIRAL ACTIVITY

Passion Pinwheel

Your passion is a vibrant energy that sets your creativity into motion. This positive energy fuels you to stretch beyond what you are comfortable with and then provides you with the strength to face any fearful, judgmental, and limiting thoughts.

Create a pinwheel to remind you of the dynamic energy available to you when you fuel yourself with passion. As you activate your pinwheel with your breath imagine the immense power of love inside you.

You will need:

The spiral page at the end of this chapter. You may want to print this onto colorful paper or card stock

Colored markers

A push pin

Scissors

A pencil with an eraser

Cut the page with the spiral so that you have a square piece with the spiral in the middle. Draw a circle the size of a quarter in the center of the spiral. Using the colored markers, write the things that you are passionate about all over the spiral.

Fold the square in half to create a triangle; you will be creating a diagonal line across the square. Then fold on the opposite diagonal so that you have an "X" shape through the spiral. Cut along the diagonal lines up to the edge of the circle at the center.

With the square facing you, pull up the right-hand edge of the bottom triangle shape and place it over the center circle. Don't flatten it. Repeat for all four triangles, holding them in place by pushing the push pin through all five layers in the center. Push the pin into the eraser of the pencil to create your pinwheel. Adjust so that the wheel can turn freely.

Activate the wheel with your breath or spin around and let the moving air spin the wheel. Find a place to put your pinwheel where the breeze can activate it freely or you can play with it easily. Try spinning around, running or dancing with your pinwheel. You may want to make several in different sizes and colors to remind you that your passions provide you with an active energy. Share them with some-one you love.

AFFIRMATION

I Am Passionate

"*My zeal for a creative life is irrepressible and I approach my work with an intensity akin to that of a head over heels infatuated lover. My earnest enthusiasm for the things I choose to embrace in life is the source of my creative powers.*"

CREATE YOUR OWN PASSIONATE AFFIRMATION

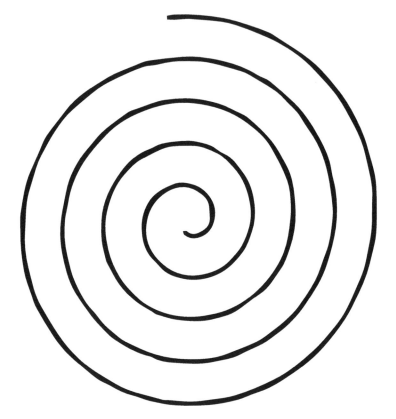

Chapter Four

Intuitive:
Claiming Our
Inner Knowing

*"The distinguishing trait of creativity is
that it requires us to reach beyond the scope
of the rational mind, toward the realm
of intuition, in order to invoke higher
consciousness and spark divine inspiration."*

Patricia Aburdene

Intuition is an intimate way of knowing. It is powerful.
It is also hard to define, yet we all have a sense of what
it is like to know something without really knowing how
we know it. This is a knowledge that is seated less in our
heads and more in our whole bodies and our hearts. It's a
physical and mysterious way of knowing often associated
with feminine, creative energy. Many of us connect our
intuition with having a gut level feeling about something.
We may think of our intuition as an internal GPS system.
Maybe you have a strong sense that something wonderful
will happen at an event you are going to and sure enough,
you meet the partner of your dreams. You let your internal
guide lead you toward your good. Perhaps you have the

feeling that you should not accept an offer to get together with someone you just met. Something just doesn't feel right. You honor your feelings and later find out that the person was involved in an illegal scam. Your intuitive radar protected you and steered you away from harm.

SHINE ON

Your Intuition

What does it mean to be intuitive? Let's take a moment to get a better sense of what intuition means to you. You may want to take a walk, sit and knit, water your garden, or watch the clouds go by. You may want to make spirals. Just let yourself be present to the moment and become aware of any information that occurs to you. Write it all down.

What does intuition mean to me?

Here is the list of concepts that have come up in my workshops. You may have come up with some similar responses. Add any of these to your own list that you like.

1. Inner Voice

2. Gut Feeling

3. Unplanned

4. Hunch

5. Spark

6. Knowing without knowing how we know

7. Mysterious connectedness

8. Spiritual

9. Feminine

10. Authentic Guidance

11. Inner Knowing

12. Unexpected

13. Out of our control

14. First inclination

15. Believe

16. Idea

17. Physical

18. Vague inkling

19. Awake

20. Bolt

21. Power Center

22. Goddess nature

With a yellow or gold marker, circle each word that resonates with you. These are your golden nuggets. They are fabulously valuable and can be considered among your greatest assets. You will want to keep them close at hand. Your creativity provides the alchemy to turn these nuggets of intuition into confidence and authentic expression.

CREATE TO RELATE

Golden Nuggets

Our intuitive powers are, by nature, hard to define and hard to put into words. We have identified some language to use when thinking about intuition. Now we will create a physical token that emphasizes the importance of our intuition.

You will need:
Yellow construction paper — two pieces of 8 ½" x 11"
Squeeze bottle glue
Gold glitter
Clear plastic zip lock bag-sandwich size
Colorful ribbon — 28" long

Cut your paper into nugget shapes that are roughly about two by three inches. Write one of your gold nugget words from the list above on each of your paper nuggets. Decorate with glue and glitter. Place your nuggets in the zip lock bag, seal it, and tie colorful ribbon around the top to cinch it up. Hang the bag somewhere you can see it often.

Is there a sound, a movement, or a color that you associate with your intuition? Can you create nuggets from drumbeats or strums? What about an intuitive dance? How else would you create an image of your intuitive nuggets?

Intuition Hosts Our Creative Process

"Cease trying to work everything out
with your minds. It will get you nowhere.
Live by intuition and inspiration and
let your whole life be a revelation."

EILEEN CADDY

Our intuition is a guide, a compass, a wise voice and a mysterious inkling. We also might think of our intuition as the milieu where our creative energy synergizes and transforms into creative action. Let's take a look at the intricate role that our intuition plays in the creative process.

It is at the intuitive level that we weave together inspiration and imagination. Inspiration is about making connections. We see or experience something from the sensory world outside of ourselves and an internal connection creates a spark. There are no limits on what we can connect to and no restrictions on where we get that spark. Often we find inspiration in unusual places. We can take advantage of that by putting ourselves in new situations and seeking out experiences that are off our well-worn paths.

Inspiration feeds our imagination. We begin to interpret the new information in our unique way and we begin seeing new connections. Inspiration and imagination begin a spiral dance together through our spirited, passionate center and that leads to a union. Something new is incubating. Over time, it will ripen into a fresh idea. That idea will glow and grow until it is fully illuminated. We may have an "Aha!" moment or the idea may simply come into clear view. This is when we begin to see our inspired idea coming to life.

Imagination now compels us to act. We set an intention that projects our idea spiraling out into the real world. We use imagination to see the completed picture and to feel the emotional energy of having made it real. We develop a plan of action that moves our inspired idea and our intention to the level of implementation. Now we do the work. We align our time, space, materials, resources, and energy with our inspired idea, and guided by our intuition we take the steps necessary to implement the plan.

Once we have implemented the idea and our new creation has come into being, we are ready to install it into its place in the world so that it may serve its purpose. If you have designed a new multimedia art center, you celebrate its installation when it is finally opened. If you have woven a baby blanket as a gift to give your daughter-in-law for your new grandbaby, the installation happens when the blanket is in the crib. When your creation has met its purpose, the step of installation completes the creative spiral for the inspired idea.

There is, however, one more phase for us as the creator. Honoring the creative cycle of birth, death, rebirth, we now experience the process of integration. All that we learned from this creative endeavor will inform the way that we work from now on. Our experience of what worked and what didn't work; the new connections that we made; the resources that we gathered, all of this has contributed to our growth. We are not the same as when we began. We are now at a new place and can begin the process anew. Each time we create, we continue to spiral ever wider and wiser.

The Intuitive Creative Process

Intuition

Inspiration

Imagination

Incubation

Illumination

Intention

Implementation

Installation

Integration

SHINE ON

Inspiration

We all have our unique experiences with finding inspiration. Often, inspiration comes to us when we are not focusing on our creative situation at all. By exploring new places, especially out of doors, we give ourselves the opportunity to make new connections.

Write about your experiences with inspiration.

1. Where do I go to get inspired?

2. What kinds of sights, sounds, smells, or experiences inspire me?

3. Are there any specific circumstances that I can choose to open myself to inspiration?

4. Are there people who inspire me? Why? What about them do I find inspiring?

A Home for Our Ahas

*"I am certain of nothing but the holiness of the
heart's affection and the truth of imagination."*

RAINER MARIE RILKE

"Aha!" you exclaim as you step dripping wet from the shower. "That's it!"

The creative muses have a habit of gracing us with inspiration at the oddest times. Toweling yourself dry, you revel in being able to see the perfect solution to your creative dilemma. You're positively giggly, as you quickly get dressed. But then the phone rings, or your teenager barges in with a desperate plea, or your dog scratches at the door and your "aha" light bulb dims. A small voice inside murmurs: "Must save idea; must save idea." What do you do?

Being the creative person that you are, you reach for your bedside journal and jot down the essence of this wonderful new idea; or you get in the car to start your carpool rounds but first you make a voice recording on your smart phone.

Living creatively requires us to be prepared to accept our "ahas" whenever they deign to come to us. A little like cats, "ahas" need to have lots of places to settle. After the creative light bulbs flash, we need to invite our "ahas" to make themselves at home so they can develop over time. For years this meant having books, boards, boxes, and binders on hand, and for some of us these tools still work great with our style of working. When an idea that has been incubating finally does hatch, now we can also use our smart phones, iPads or laptops or save our ideas as a voice recording. Most of us hardly go anywhere without snapping photos and we have amazing tools for working with images at our fingertips.

Twyla Tharp in her book *The Creative Habit: Learn it and Use it for Life* tells us that she begins every new choreography project with an ordinary filing box. She begins gathering up the things that she will need including inspiring images, props, music etc and then labels the box. "It makes it real," she tells us.

Once a creative idea begins to evolve in our mind's eye, we can nurture it by collecting physical tokens of our developing vision. You may want to use a physical board or computer to visually organize your ideas. Make a collage of pictures, text, and drawings to create a visual of your inspired idea. This kind of board serves two purposes: it's a gathering place for the elements of our unfolding dream, and because it is mostly visual, it's also a stimulant to our subconscious and right brain creative juices.

For those of us who are really hands-on, boxes, boards, and binders are great for organizing. Touching the materials and being able to move them, group them, and manipulate them can be an important part of the process. More visual folks will find the tools for organizing on a laptop, iPad, or phone; they work well and are very portable.

SHINE ON

Capturing Inspiration

Be prepared. The Boy Scout's motto makes sense for us in our creative adventures. Take some time to reflect on your creative preparedness. Ask yourself:

1. How do I capture my inspiration?

2. In what ways do I provide a welcome home for inspiration?

3. What can I do from now on to be sure that I can take advantage of inspiration when it comes?

Accessing Our Intuitive Powers

"…we need to pay exquisite attention to our responses to things — noticing what makes our flame grow brighter. If we pay attention to those things, we'll be able to catch the flame and feed it."

NINA SIMONS

Living intuitively requires making a space for ourselves to listen. Today's media-driven world has us sitting in front of screens for more and more hours every day. We are bombarded with information in a nonstop stream 24/7, and our inner voice just can't compete with that. So what can we do to turn the volume down on the outside din and tune in to our voice within? Spending time reconnecting with the natural world is essential to honing our intuitive skills. Open the door and step out. Let yourself become a curious observer.

Take a look around and listen. Breathe in the world around you. Let your senses come out to play. The natural world speaks to us with a language all its own: the ebb and flow of the tides, the changing seasons, or the stars in the night sky. Drink it in. Take a walk around the block, go to a park, a garden, the beach, or a river. You don't have to go far to look up at the sky and let the clouds feed your imagination.

Nature's lessons are plentiful. Your intuition hones in on just the right element for your body, mind, and heart to make a connection with your unique work. Slow your pace, be curious, open wide and receive what nature has to offer.

I live on a wooded acre just outside of Santa Barbara so when I step out my door the lessons begin. Walking up to my studio one afternoon, I saw a beautiful snake skin sticking out of a hole on the side of the driveway. The shed skin was about three feet long and very much intact. It occurred to me that the gopher snake had been able to free herself of the old shell as she descended down into the darkness. That thought resounded in me like a special-delivery message from the universe. I had been consciously trying to tune into my inner voice, and listen to my inner guides, and I knew that it was time for me to "shed" some old habits that did not serve my art making.

SHINE ON

Lessons from Nature

Turn off your devices and walk away. Find a spot where you can be connected with nature. Sit quietly if that feels right, or walk, surf, hike or bike. Engage all of your senses. Dig in the dirt, rake leaves, go fishing or daydream in your hammock. Invite nature to speak to you. Listen intuitively. Use your journal to record what you learn.

What do you hear nature sharing with you?

CREATE TO RELATE

Sensory Spiral Meditation Cards

Spending time in nature is one way to connect us with our intuition. But don't worry our intuitive powers don't stop when we step inside. It can be a challenge to disconnect from our busy lives and create a space for exploring intuition. We can practice connecting with our intuitive source by using the spiral in simple rituals that we can easily weave into our daily routines. The more we bring our awareness to how our thoughts and emotions resonate in our bodies, the better we understand our own intuitive skills.

In this Create to Relate activity we will be creating a special set of spiral cards that will engage your senses of smell, touch, and sight, strengthening your body's connection to your intuitive wisdom. You can use the cards as a way to center yourself, to tune into your inner guidance, or to invite a sense of calm serenity. You may also use them as a starting ritual for your creative work. I keep my set on my writing desk and use them as a way to settle into my writing sessions.

You will need:

Card stock paper

Glue in a squeezable bottle with a tip.

A variety of things with distinct textures and smells which could be things like salt, sand, coffee grounds, rice, birdseed, beads, ground spices, feathers, cotton balls, twine, yarn, or anything that can be glued to the card in a spiral.

Cut several pieces of card stock into eight and a half inch squares. Each card will have a spiral with a different texture.

Using a squeeze bottle of glue, create a sticky spiral that fills the card. Pour one of the following over the card to create a textured spiral:

- Salt. Could be table salt, coarse salt, sea salt. You may want to try several different salt textures.

- Birdseed

- Rice, quinoa or any other kind of uncooked grain

- Coffee grounds. Could be instant coffee, which will melt into the glue, or coarse grounds of different types and smells.

- Dirt or sand

- Seed beads

- Coarsely ground spices like pepper, cinnamon, dill leaves etc.

- Cotton ball fluff. Pull apart the cotton ball and glue down the tufts

- Yarn, twine, rope. Use a variety of textures

Cover the glue with the textured stuff, tip the card to be sure that all of the glue is covered and let the extra fall off the card. Set to dry. Create six to ten different cards to make your set. You can store them in a box or large envelope.

To use the cards as a tool for centering, place a card in front of you on the table. Quiet yourself. Place your finger at the opening of the spiral and slowly trace the pathway into the center. Stop and focus on your breath for one deep inhale and exhale.

Trace your way back out of the spiral.

For Variety: Close your eyes and feel your way through the spiral pathway. Use the empty space or trace the textured curving line. Use each different finger on both hands, alternating either after each inward and outward trace is complete. Or spiral in with one finger and spiral out with another.

Inhale the scent of that card and let your mind free associate with that smell.

Ask your inner self a question as you trace the spiral inward. Then, listen as you trace the spiral outward. Repeat as desired.

Imagination and Intention

Imagine what you want to manifest in your life. By creating a vision of what it is you would like to manifest, you are creating a road map to your dreams. Visualization is a powerful tool, and adding in the emotional component makes visualizing even more effective.

Imagine what it will feel like to have your dreams come true. Then you can make a statement of intention that points you in the right direction. This is not a magic ride; it is more like holding a light up so you can see your pathway and make decisions along the way.

Setting an intention is like painting a picture of your hearts desire. You project out an image of what it is that you want. You add in the feelings that are associated with the fulfillment of that desire. Then you take whatever actions will make your dream come true. Here are some guidelines for setting an intention:

- Get a clear picture of what it is you want and then state it clearly in the present tense.

- Imagine how you will feel if your desire is already manifest and express those feelings as if you were already experiencing the end result.

- Take action to move toward the end goal.

- Be open, stay aware, and practice gratitude.

Here is a sample intention:

"I am so full of joy and gratitude as I share my book with others. I love the way the book looks, and I enjoy sending it out into the world. I am honored and grateful that, because of my book, I am frequently asked to teach at conferences and for groups and I am enjoying my interactions and collaborations with many creative people."

~~~

SHINE ON

Set an Intention

Now it's your turn. Set an intention for your next creative project. Write your intention on a card that you can look at and read several times a day. Begin with an "I" statement and write in the present tense. Include the feelings that you wish to experience when the intention is fulfilled and an expression of gratitude. Let your words create a vibrant scenario of what it will be like when you have accomplished this goal.

It's not enough to just write out your intention and then put it aside and wait for something to happen. You must put your intention into motion with your actions. In the next chapter you will create and implement a plan for turning your intentions into reality.

While we are still focusing on our intuitive powers, let's employ the use of metaphor for setting our intention in motion. You can recite your intention out loud as you use the Sensory Spiral Mediation Cards that you made earlier in this chapter. You can reinforce the intention that you set by making it a part of your Create to Relate activity and the Spiral activity.

CREATE TO RELATE

Walk Your Talk

"Without
The silence of nature within
The power within, the power without.
The path is whatever passes, no end in itself.
The end is grace, ease,
Healing, not saving.
Singing the proof,
The proof of the power within."

GARY SNYDER

The practice of walking in a spiral pathway has been used across cultures as a form of meditation and as a way of slowing down to listen deeply to our intuitive wisdom. The movement through the spiral path is a metaphor for going inward to access our inner resources; and the path outward represents our expression of creativity in the world. Complex labyrinths have been designed throughout history for this purpose, but you can easily create a very simple spiral path that you can use at your own home space.

Think of all of the ways that you can create a walking spiral to use near your home or work. Create the spiral in a driveway, patio, playground, or any outdoor area. Make it big enough to walk in and out of. You can use sidewalk chalk on cement, birdseed on grass, or simply draw the spiral with a stick in the dirt. Look around to see what nature has to offer you as materials. You might use small pebbles, sticks, leaves, or shells. Making the spiral can become part of the meditation.

Take a deep breath and enter the spiral, slowly following the path to the center. Think about the intention that you have set for your current project, or you may want to stay open to inspiration. Stop in the center of the spiral and allow yourself to be aware of the present moment. Tune in to all of your senses. Walk the pathway outward. Stop when you are done and again center yourself in the present moment. Repeat as often as you like.

SPIRAL ACTIVITY

Setting Your Intention in Motion

Make a copy of the spiral at the end of the chapter for each intention that you want to set. Write your intention in first person, including an expression of gratitude into the spiral. Use your color-makers to decorate the spiral and enhance its vibrancy. Then cut out the spiral following the lines into the center. As you lift your cut spiral from the center, see how it begins to move, pulsing and twirling. Punch a hole in the center of the spiral and, using a piece of string, hang it in a place where you can see your intention metaphorically set into motion.

You may want to also write out your intention on a card to keep near your bed so that you can read it when you awake in the morning and again before you go to sleep at night.

I Am Intuitive

"My pure natural sensitivity to my world inspires and guides me to what I want to express and how to express it. I rely on my visceral, spontaneous perception of what inherently works for me and I feed my imagination by choosing new experiences."

CREATE YOUR OWN INTUITIVE AFFIRMATION

CREATE YOUR INTENTION

Chapter Five

Real Creative Living

*"Balance and stillness coexist as opposites.
Stillness alone is the potentiality for creativity.*

*Movement alone is creativity restricted to a
certain aspect of expression.*

*But the combination of movement and
stillness is creativity unleashed in all directions
wherever the power of intention takes you."*

DEEPAK CHOPRA

In our creative spiral journey, we have reached the pivotal point where we have explored our way into the center of our hearts and souls. Now we begin to focus outward. This is where all of our inner awareness and our growth come to play in establishing the daily routines that support the manifestation of our outer creative lives. It's time to get real.

Our creative life doesn't just happen. There is much to manage as we endeavor to create a life that is full of spirit. Our authentic expression of love requires time, energy, and resources in order to spiral outward into the world. As we have in each chapter, let's first take a look at how you experience the concept "real."

SHINE ON

What Does Real Mean to You?

What comes to mind for you when you think of the word "real?" What does it take to make your dreams come true?

Ask yourself: What does it mean to make something real? What real life concepts are involved in manifesting my intentions? Take as much time as you need. You may want to carry the concept of "real" around with you while you go about your day. Take notes, record your thoughts on your phone, or just let the concept marinate. Then, when you have a quiet moment, write down everything that has come to you relating to "real."

Here are some of the words that have come up in my workshops:

Visible, tangible, present, planned, unmasked, grounded, connected, in time and space, audible, sensory, realistic, action-oriented, directed, cyclical, finances, goals, spontaneous, stuff, place to create, structure.

You may want to add some of these to your list as well to get a well-rounded picture of what factors come into play to bring your vision into reality.

Write across the top of a page in your journal: *Body, Spirit, Passion, Intuition, World.*

Sort through your "real" words and list them under each heading where you think they fit. Notice that a word may fit under several or even all of the headings. Be aware of the connections that are made and your thoughts and feelings as you do this activity.

What did you find? How does making something real involve your spirit, passion, and intuition as well as your physical presence in the world? Use this chart as a reminder that you can integrate your various sources of wisdom and apply your whole self to bringing your imagined goals into being.

SPIRITED Goals

"What you get by achieving your goals is not as important as what you become by achieving your goals."
HENRY DAVID THOREAU

When you formed your creative idea into an intention, you set in motion the creative process for implementation. The next step is to create a specific goal and a plan to implement the steps that will move you toward the completion of your goal. Setting a goal extends the energy of your intention by adding in the specific details of what you want to accomplish and in what time frame. Your plan will break your goal down into the action steps that you will need to take to create results.

Many of us have experience setting goals. You may have set annual New Year resolutions to lose weight or imagined yourself vacationing on a tropical island. Perhaps you have set financial goals or goals to change your health. You may have achieved some of your goals, or you may have never seen any results after setting your goal.

How can we set goals that propel us toward our vision of what we want to create? You will be more likely to succeed in achieving a goal when you engage your imagination, your intuition, your passion, and your spirit. One popular structuring tool that you may have encountered for goal setting, involves the acronym SMART, which stands for: Specific, Measurable, Achievable, Realistic, and Time-oriented. There are many resources online for using SMART goals. I used this tool in my workshops for years, weaving in a focus on heart and soul. But SMART goals do not include our most powerful assets.

Now, I have created a way to integrate the savvy of the SMART goals with the internal powers of the individual by using SPIRITED as my acronym for goal setting. Here is what a SPIRITED goal entails.

- *Specific:* Is it clearly defined and measurable?

- *Passion-based:* Am I in love with this goal?

- *Intuitive:* Does this goal feel as though it is in alignment with your spirit?

- *Realistic:* Is this goal achievable?

- *Imaginative:* Am I bringing my creative powers to this goal?

- *Time-based:* Can I set a time line for this goal?

- *Expansive:* Does this goal move me toward my vision of success, joy or fulfillment?

- *Discovery-based:* Does this goal give me an opportunity to discover and learn new skills, or provide personal growth?

Let's look at how to turn an intention into a SPIRITED goal. Here is the intention that I shared in the last chapter:

"I am so full of joy and gratitude as I share my book with others. I love the way the book looks and feels, and I enjoy sending it out into the world. I am honored and grateful that because of my book, I am frequently asked to teach at conferences and for groups and I am enjoying my interactions and collaborations with many creative people."

This intention paints an emotional picture of the life that I would like to experience after publishing my book. There are actually three different goals that are inherent in this intention:

1. To publish my book.

2. To teach the concepts from the book at conferences and to groups.

3. To form creative collaborations based on being the author of the book.

For this example I will focus on writing a SPIRITED goal for publishing the book. Following the guidelines outlined above, I begin by creating a specific clearly defined and measurable statement of what I want to accomplish. Then modify my statement, adding to it until it fully embodies all of the elements of a SPIRITED goal. Here is the step-by-step process:

Specific: My goal is to publish my book.

I will know that this is accomplished when I have the book printed and am holding it in my hand.

Passion-based: I am passionate about publishing my book. By adding in my strong feelings I am clarifying the role my heart will play in accomplishing this goal.

Intuitive: I am passionately committed to publishing my book. YES. This feels right to me and I am willing to commit myself to this goal.

Realistic: I am passionately committed to applying all of my resources, including my ability to write, my editing and marketing skills, and my finances; and to getting help from professionals so that I can follow through on each step necessary to publish my book.

Here, I outline what I will need to achieve this goal. I determine whether this is realistic based on my ability to follow through on the book-making process. Please note that this step includes an element of faith. Even though I have never published a book before, I believe that this goal is realistic. I also have support from others who have published books and who have encouraged me to go for it.

Imaginative: I am passionately committed to sharing my book with the world. I see myself applying all of my creative resources to publishing the book including: my ability to write, my editing and marketing skills, and my finances. I enjoy getting help from professionals so that I can follow through on each step necessary to make my book real. I love the way the book looks and feels, and I enjoy sending it out into the world.

I will use the power of my imagination to visualize each step of this process and to imagine the completed goal. I imagine the physical sensations of holding and reading the book.

Time-based: I am passionately committed to sharing my book with the world by June 1, 2014. I see myself applying all of my creative resources to publishing the book including: my ability to write, my editing and marketing skills, and my finances. I enjoy getting help from professionals so that I can follow through on each step necessary to make my book real. I love the way the book looks and feels, and I enjoy sending it out into the world.

Setting a specific date gives me a timeline to work from. This date is not set in stone, but it helps me to plan my time and resources. I can do some research to get a sense of how long the different steps in the process might take. I remain flexible but I also have a desire to complete my goal in the time frame that I have set. The time frame may change as the project progresses.

Expansive: I am passionately committed to sharing my book with the world by June 1, 2014. I see myself applying all of my creative resources to publishing the book including: my ability to write, my editing and marketing skills, and my finances. I enjoy getting help from professionals so that I can follow through on each step necessary to make my book real. I am so full of joy and gratitude as I share my book with others. I love the way the book looks and feels, and enjoy sending it out into the world.

Completing this goal of publishing my book fills me with a joyful sense of expansion as I imagine myself sharing it with people all over the world.

Discovery-based: I am passionately committed to sharing my book with the world by June 1, 2014. I see myself applying all of my creative resources to publishing the book including: my ability to write, my editing and marketing skills, and my finances. I look forward to learning about the publishing process and I am open to making many new discoveries along my way. I enjoy getting help from professionals so that I can follow through on each step necessary to make my book real. I am so full of joy and gratitude as I share my book with others. I love the way the book looks and feels, and enjoy sending it out into the world.

The final goal statement aligns spirit, passion, and intuition. It includes a physical sensibility, imagination and openness. It is time-specific, measurable, realistic, and exciting. This goal resonates with me in many ways and motivates me to create a plan of action that is going to become a significant part of my creative journey.

Using this tool for setting goals expands the breadth of our engagement with the process of creating something that has not existed before. Every time we set a goal, we are making our way toward the unknown. By including all of our sources of wisdom and power in our goal setting, we support our chances of successful completion and enhance the enjoyment and fulfillment that we experience as we move toward the vision that we have in mind.

〜〜

SHINE ON

Setting Your SPIRITED Goal

The process of setting a SPIRITED goal helps you to identify and clarify your desires and align your spirit, heart, and intuitive senses to open the flow of energy in the direction you want to go. Use this guide for setting a SPIRITED goal. You can use one of the intentions that you set in the last chapter or create a new intention. Follow the above example and build the goal, step by step. You may want to take notes on the side of any feelings and body sensations that you become aware of as you answer some of the questions included here. They are designed to help you experience a full understanding of why you are setting this goal and why it will motivate you to action.

> *Specific:* What do I specifically want to accomplish? What will that look and feel like? How will I know that I have met this goal? What tangible evidence will there be?

110

Passion-based: What do I love about this goal? What about this goal brings me joy? What parts of the process of meeting this goal will be the most fun? How will I intentionally incorporate my passions into working toward this goal?

Intuitive: What is it about this goal that feels the most true for me? How will I feel when I am on track? Off track?

Realistic: Have I clearly assessed that my goal is achievable? Do I believe that this is possible? What will be my biggest obstacles?

Imaginative: What is the most creative part of this goal? How will I use my imagination to reach my goal? What are the unique features of this goal?

Time-based: What is my timeline for this goal? When do I want to have completed this goal? When will I know that it has been met?

Expansive: How will this goal stretch or challenge me to grow? What will I need to change about myself, or my choices while working on this goal? What will be different in me, and my life after I reach this goal?

Discovery-based: Am I open to exploring unknown territory? Am I willing to learn new skill sets? What do I think I might discover?

You now have a well-rounded picture of what your goal is and what it will be like for you as you live the movement toward your goal. Remember that the structure that your SPIRITED goal provides is not supposed to be poured in cement. It's supposed to resonate with you like a beautiful chime or remind you of a tree with its roots in solid ground that bends and moves in the wind. Fueled by passion and powered by your intuition, you can incorporate your personal style into the process of making something real that never existed before you imagined it.

SASSIE Plans

"You can't plan an inspired life."
TAMA KIEVES

When Tama Kieves finished her talk at the Women's International Festival in Santa Barbara, I literally ran to the back table where she was headed to sign her books. Her personal testimony and encouragement to live the "life you love" had set me on fire. I immediately vowed to be standing on stage sharing my own book one day.

After thanking her for signing my new copy of her book I went home to start living my inspired life. This book is the result of that passionate vow, and the tools I'm sharing here are ones that I found truly helpful. They combine the intuitive awareness that is so essential for us to open to inspiration and suggestions for actions that support our creative ability to manifest our intentions.

I find that planning is an integral part of the creative process. Yes, plans can go awry, and there is an element of risk even when we plan. But, once you have set your SPIRITED goal, creating an action plan helps to clarify the daily choices that you will need to sort through. We are not carving anything in stone. The plans we formulate are not meant to be rigid but more like a dance between structure and flow, a fluid concept, meant as an aid to help us develop a daily routine that leads us through our goals and becomes our fulfilling life.

In my workshops I like to introduce the idea of making a SASSIE plan. The word "sassy" means bold, lively, jaunty, or even cheeky and this word sets the tone for a plan that has spunk. I like the implication that plans can be spunky instead of staid or formal. I use SASSIE as an acronym, that outlines the steps to help you to keep the flow going. See how this becomes a spiral of action, energized by your passionate energy and intuitive wisdom.

How does the acronym SASSIE help us to take action on our goals? Here is how this planning tool outlines the steps we need to follow:

Set a SPIRITED goal

Assess where I am now. What strengths and skills do I have to support me? What do I need in order to take the first/next step? Who and what can I use as resources?

Specify the steps by creating a plan.

Schedule the time and create the space

Implement the plan. Take action!

Evaluate. What is working? What have I learned? What do I need to change?

You will spiral through these steps over and over again as you complete each phase of your plan. You will circle back to reassess where you are and what you need, and determine what the next step will be, what your timeline will be, and what specific actions that you need to take. Every time you move forward, you will evaluate your progress and make any needed adjustments.

What would this look like for the goal that I set to self-publish my book? Let's go through the process together. I have specifically set my SPIRITED goal, so let's start with the next step that is represented by the letter "A." Here is where I get a good idea of where I am now in the process. I can use my journal to keep track of this assessment understanding that this will also be a record of my progress.

Assess: For my assessment of where I am now, I might write: All of the writing is done. I have worked with an editor and now have a completed manuscript. I'm working with a consultant to help me with the cover design. I have an image that I want to use and I've written the text for the back cover. I know a web designer who will help me create a web site to accompany my book. I need to talk to my consultant about things like how to get an ISBN number and about the printing process. I need to find out whom to contact to create simple illustrations for my book. I'll talk to my consultant and create a timeline and action plan.

Specify: To specify the steps in my plan, I will need to outline all of the steps involved in printing the book. I need help with this since I have never done this before. So my first step will be to schedule a meeting with my consultant. I'll ask about what else I need to do in order to move forward. I'll find out about printing costs and the cost of illustrations. I need to research what my choices are. I'll ask for help finding the right printing company and see what services they offer.

Schedule: Here is where I schedule my time. That might look like this: Meet with consultant next Tuesday at noon. Get questions answered and research done by the following Tuesday.

Implement: Implementing the plan involves showing up at the scheduled meeting and spending time researching.

Evaluate: After my meeting, I will take what I have learned and set new specific steps. I'll make adjustments to my timeline as I find out from the various different services about their timelines to do the work.

At the end of the week, I will want to assess where I am in the process again and continue to adapt the plan. Making changes and adjustments becomes a natural part of the process. As we move forward, new possibilities will appear, and our idea will grow and evolve. So the implementation of our plan is a fluid process. Here is where we can use guidelines that are flexible enough to allow us the freedom to change and make adjustments, but offers us enough structure to actually help us create actions that are effective.

The adjustments that we need to make will not all be action-related. We will be experiencing a myriad of thoughts and emotions as we stretch into each phase of creating something new. We can practice the self-love that we explored in Chapter Three by reminding ourselves to let go of judgment and perfection and by encouraging ourselves to choose acceptance and gentle self-love. We can support our growth by acknowledging our progress, and being aware of our daily successes. Then, we can celebrate each of our accomplishments along the way.

SHINE ON
Making a SASSIE plan

In the last chapter, you set intentions to project your creative vision outward toward fulfillment. In this chapter, you learned about turning that intention into a SPIRITED goal. Next, you learned how to create a SASSIE plan to help you take the needed action to bring your dream to life. Here is your chance to practice making a SASSIE plan for your SPIRITED goal. Write out your goal. Follow the SASSIE acronym to create your plan.

Center yourself by asking yourself: What will it look and feel like when I have met this goal? This will bring you back to your intention.

Now you can use these tools to move toward making your intention real. Keep in mind that our creativity benefits from steps but will choreograph our movements in curving, swirling, twisting patterns that allow for opportunities for us to grow in many directions. Even when the intention has been set, the goals clearly defined, and the steps planned out, we will need to continually spiral inward to center ourselves in our love and intuition.

Procrastination:
Making Peace with the Process

"Until one is committed, there is hesitancy, the chance to draw back. Concerning all acts of initiative (and creation), there is one elementary truth, the ignorance of which kills countless ideas and splendid plans: that the moment one definitely commits oneself, then Providence moves too. All sorts of things occur to help one that would never otherwise have occurred. A whole stream of events issues from the decision, raising in one's favor all manner of unforeseen incidents and meetings and material assistance, which no man could have dreamed would have come his way. Whatever you can do, or dream you can do, begin it. Boldness has genius, power, and magic in it. Begin it now."

WILLIAM HUTCHINSON MURRAY

Even when we feel as though we are finally moving in the right direction and we anticipate the good things that await us, we may put off doing the things that we know are the next step toward achieving our goals. We wake up scheduled to do two hours of writing on our memoir, and suddenly, cleaning the refrigerator becomes our top priority. We plan to call several galleries to make appointments to show our work, but instead we spend all morning chatting on the phone with old high school chums that we just had to reconnect with. Most of the time, it doesn't take a psychiatrist to figure out what is going on. We are procrastinating.

There are many reasons why we put off taking the steps in our SASSIE plans to reach our SPIRITED goals. Taking the time to bring our awareness and acceptance to what we are thinking, and feeling gives us the opportunity to make new choices as we honor our experience of the whole spectrum of the creative process. Often times, we can move past our procrastination by finding out what we need and allowing ourselves to access it.

For example, sometimes we just don't have all of the information or resources that we need to move ahead. If this is the case, we can take a moment to identify what information we need and make a plan to get it. We can ask for help. Many of us get stuck reinventing the wheel when we could easily find what we need already waiting for us. On the other hand, we may find that we have *too much* information, and it feels overwhelming or even impossible to sort through and to find what is useful and meaningful.

Feeling overwhelmed can be extremely uncomfortable, so putting off our goals seems like a good alternative. But centering ourselves in love and gently bringing acceptance to these feelings helps us to find the courage to look for solutions. Here is where we spiral back to trusting in our intuition, connecting with our body, and centering ourselves in love.

There are tools and techniques that we can use to help us to move past our sense of overwhelm. For example, we can break down large tasks into smaller steps. Taking one small step at a time allows us to move at our own authentic pace and to enjoy ourselves as we go along. An added bonus to taking one step at a time is that we are more able to listen to our hearts and be open to celebrating our small successes.

Making a schedule and using the technique of back tracking can be very helpful. If we are creating work for a deadline, we can start at the deadline to determine what needs to be done, and then make a plan of action for each week leading up to the deadline. By back tracking, we can easily see what we should focus on each day or week in order to accomplish our goal. We will be able to schedule our time and reduce the stress of meeting the deadline by working step-by-step, toward the finished project.

Deep breathing, meditation, or visualizations will help us keep a body/mind/soul connection. We can use our spirals to center us, and our affirmations to shift our feelings and energy. Here is an affirmation for dealing with feelings of overwhelm:

"Today I will take one small step toward my goal. I celebrate my progress and trust in the timing."

Sometimes we procrastinate because we have lost interest in our goal. Things may have changed to the point that we no longer feel the passion for this goal. You may need to ask yourself: Does this still have meaning for me? When we listen with our body, heart and spirit we will know whether we have moved past this goal or if there is something else going on that we need to shine a light on and address.

SHINE ON

Procrastination

Can you think of an instance when you procrastinated instead of taking the actions that you needed to manifest your goal? Describe what was going on for you. Include details of how your body felt, and what thoughts you were entertaining.

Real Fear

*"Human beings have the awesome ability
to take any experience of their lives and
create a meaning that dis-empowers them
or one that literally can save their lives."*
ANTHONY ROBBINS

Our fears are real and they provide an important mechanism that helps us to navigate our life. Fear is a natural and organic emotion. We can learn to allow our fears to be a part of our life, yet not limit or control our life choices. We began to get familiar with our fears as we explored our passionate love center. The more familiar our fears are to us, the less they waylay us. So we practice bringing our awareness, our acceptance and our love to our fears and using the techniques we learned in Chapter Three. In this chapter we will look at a couple of specific sources of fear and some tools for shifting our energy when we are faced with these common feelings.

Many creative people fear failure. This may mean failing according to some outward standard, like not being accepted by your first choice art school, being rejected by a book publisher, or not being able to create the flower arrangement that you see in your mind's eye. Changing your perspective to embrace the adventure of entering into the unknown may help to shift the energy around these events. Also, changing your language when you think and speak about taking risks can help you to remain centered in self-acceptance.

Each time we risk putting our work out into the world, or allowing ourselves to take a step out of our comfort zones, we can assure ourselves that we are in the creative process. Some of what we try will work brilliantly, and some will not work at all. We know that ahead of time, and we can see that each step along the way is necessary for our creative unfolding. We can affirm that we are okay with whatever the results of our efforts are, because we will have learned something that will become a part of our overall body of knowledge and experience. Sometimes we feel disappointed, but we can acknowledge that, let it go, and get back on track.

While we are getting familiar with our fear of failure, we may discover that some of our fearful feelings actually have to do with our thoughts about success. The fear of success is often linked to our attitudes about change, risk, or exploring the unknown. That is why it is so common for creative people to experience this fear. We are all on the pathway that takes us through the unknown. Embracing healing and growth are essential parts of our creative journey.

As we align our hearts, minds, bodies, and spirits with acceptance and compassion, we can examine our beliefs about change. By bringing awareness to these underlying beliefs, we can journal about our pictures of success as well as our need for transitions. Then we can imagine new possibilities.

SHINE ON

Fear of Failure and Fear of Success

Part 1: Often, reminding ourselves of our successes boosts our resolve for taking risks. When our fear of failure threatens to limit us, then it's time to shine a light on our accomplishments for fortification.

Write out ten situations when you felt successful. As you write, visualize each situation and the feelings of joy and accomplishment that you felt. This doesn't have to be winning the Nobel Peace Prize. Choose times when you took a risk and everything turned out well. Remind yourself of how your energy shifted from the fear of the unknown result, to the joy of successful completion. Tune in to your body and the sensations of success. What does success feel like?

Part 2: Write out the thoughts that you have after reading through the following questions:

1. How do you think that your success will change your relationships, your home life, or your work life?

2. Is there anything that keeps you from being able to feel the joy and celebration of your accomplishments?

Be sure to shine a light on any minimizing myths that you have regarding success that need to shift. Write affirmations that you can use to create a new, positive image of how you may experience success. Read them out loud and let the words resonate in your heart and body.

༄

CREATE TO RELATE

Celebrate Success

Take one of your most gratifying successes and make yourself an award that represents your internal satisfaction. This recognition is an acknowledgment that you followed your authentic inner compass and succeeded in overcoming your fear. You showed some true gumption and earned a badge of courage.

Get creative with this. Use fancy paper to create a certificate or you can fashion a trophy from recycled bottles. Use gold paint, glitter, or sparkles to embellish your award, if you like. Be sure it states your accomplishment. Present it to yourself in a fun and dramatic ceremony. Accept it with gratitude and joy. Display it and view it whenever you feel like success eludes you.

Spiral back to your passionate heart center and bring self-acceptance and love to your tendency to hold back. When fear happens, let it be a part of your creative journey of deeper self-discovery. Then move forward, knowing that you have some good tools for support.

You may want to make a representation of your fear of failure or your fear of success to put into the fear sanctuary that you made in Chapter Three. Be sure to tell your fears that you accept them as you place them into the safety of the sanctuary.

Making Peace with Time and Space

"How did it get so late so soon?"
Dr. Seuss

When I ask my coaching clients what they find the most challenging in following their creative path, they very often state that they don't have enough time to create. It serves us to shine a light on our relationship with time in our day-to-day choice making. A wonderful resource for looking at time in creative ways is the book *Creating Time: Using Creativity to Reinvent the Clock and Reclaim your Life*, by Marney K. Makridakis. The author invites us to use writing, art, and ritual to see time in new ways. I particularly enjoyed the idea of creating a "Time Guide." Makridakis suggests that, when we personify time, we can learn to build our trust in time.

Making peace with time involves making conscious choices and aligning our actions with our SPIRITED goals. This requires that we pay attention to how we make choices. Does what you do support who you want to be and what you desire to create?

SHINE ON

Your Relationship with Time

Bring your awareness to your perception about time as a concept. Check in to see if you have any beliefs that are minimizing myths for you. Write down all the feelings and associations that you have about time. Then, ask yourself the following questions and write out your thoughts.

1. What do I believe to be true about time and my creative work?

2. How much time do I spend each week doing things that serve what I'm passionate about?

3. How do I experience time when I am working?

4. What are my challenges in relationship to time and my creative goals?

5. Is there anything that I can change to improve my mastery of time?

6. Are there any tasks I now do that I could delegate to someone else?

7. What are these tasks, and who can help me?

8. Are there any obligations that I could let go of to make room for more creative time?

Spirit, Time and Ritual

"Any ritual is an opportunity for transformation."
SKYHAWK

The thoughts and feelings that we have about time impact the way we structure our creative work. Sometimes we may want to bypass our conscious thoughts, especially if they are negative or fearful. When we connect with our spirit instead, we find that our minimizing myths, automatic negative thoughts, and our fears don't prevent us from using the full power of the creative process to activate our dreams.

How do we connect directly with our spirit or soul? Here we will once again turn to the practice of ritual. Throughout the history of humankind, people have created rituals that work at a deep level to trigger a soul response. We use rituals to engage us in a sensual, physical, mental, emotional and spiritual way.

We can use rituals to get us started on a project, to help us maintain our focus, to support our decision-making, and to celebrate our successes. We creative types often fall in love with the thrill of starting a new project. Playing with the ideas, gathering the materials, and the joy of that first bit of creative activity really tickles us. But how often do we run out of steam and set that project aside in order to start something new and feel the rush of excitement again? How can we continually show up to do the work, even when our initial enthusiasm has faded?

Creating a ritual way of beginning our work each day can make all the difference in our ability to happily complete what we have begun. A starting ritual aligns our spirit, mind, body and emotions to support our creative work. It helps us to bypass any objections that come up and moves us into the creative zone. Like turning the key in the ignition of a car, a ritual can help to turn on the creative flow, regardless of our mood.

When creating a starting ritual, you should take into account the setting where you work. Rituals are best when they engage you with as many of your senses as possible and set a mood that is conducive to focusing on your creative tasks. You can begin your ritual as you enter your workspace, whether it is a kitchen table, spare bedroom, or professional studio.

I like to use the mantra "Breathe. Center. Enter." Taking a deep breath, I walk into the center of a large spiral that I have drawn in chalk in front of my studio door.

Drawing spirals can be used as a starting ritual, and so can tracing the spiral cards that we made with the textures and smells. Lighting a scented candle and putting on soft music before we sit down to work can create a productive mood. Doing a set of simple stretches or movements engages the whole body. We might take a moment to close our eyes and invoke the muses before we begin, or simply stating out loud, "It's a glorious day to create!"

Once you have decided on your starting ritual, it is essential that you do it every time you begin to work. The ritual opens the door for us to be fully present to our creative task. Experts say that it takes about thirty days to create a new habit. Even if you don't do your work every day, it will help for you to use the same ritual consistently. Then, even on the days that you're not feeling particularly inspired, performing your starting ritual can get the creative juices flowing and spark an automatic response.

Designing a Starting Ritual

Let your senses and imagination guide you to just the right ritual for you. Play with different ways of entering your space. Try setting a timer and letting the sound be your prompt. Engage your sense of smell with a lavender sachet or a spritz of lemon water.

What kind of starting ritual will you create in order to prompt your creative juices to flow? Write out the details of your ritual. Perform it and see if it engages you. Create a practice of using your starting ritual daily or whenever you begin your work.

Honoring Our Creative Time

"Creativity really only needs space and time,
two of the hardest gifts to give yourself."
Sara Rauch

When we honor our creative work and recognize its importance to our lives, we find that creating time to work comes naturally. Still, it can be a challenge to piece together all of the commitments in our busy lives with family, friends, jobs, and community. One of the things that we can take a look at is how many times we say "Yes" to requests for our time, leaving less available time for our creative work.

Learning to say "no" when people ask you for some of your time can be challenging. We want to be nice. We want to do it all. We want to be a part of the community. There are many things you may want, but at some point you need to ask yourself an important question: Does saying "yes" to this support my Spirited, Passionate, Intuitive, Real, Authentic Life?

Gail McMeekin, in her book, *The Power of Positive Choices: Adding and Subtracting Your Way to a Great Life,* suggests we identify our priorities and then subtract everything that distracts us from achieving our goals. This will support us in the positive choices we can make in our creative lives. "The power of subtraction is astounding," according to McMeekin because saying "no" to the things that limit us opens up space for the things that we want more of.

Many of us have been led to believe that we are the hub of the wheel and that our family and community could not function without us. I'm not suggesting that you are not extremely valuable, but I am suggesting it does not serve us to think that we alone must do it all. The truth is that we do not have to do it all. We can step back from a long list of tasks and find that the world continues to spin on its axis. We can choose how we want to spend our time, what we want to contribute to, what is important to us, and what we want to say "yes" to.

The work that you did identifying your values and your passions will help you to stay centered. Choose those people, things and circumstances that support you, nurture you and bring you joy, peace and a sense of wholeness.

SHINE ON

Saying No

Saying "no" when we are asked to contribute time and energy to a friend, our family, or our community can be a difficult choice. Even when we are very clear about our SPIRITED goals, feel passionate about our work, and are using the tools that support us, we still might feel uncomfortable about saying "no" and claiming our time for our creative work. One way to honor both yourself and the person with the request for your time is to approach your answer from a different perspective. The way that you frame your response can make a big difference. I suggest you try saying something like this:

"Thank you so much for thinking of me. I'm honored. I'm going to pass on this opportunity and let someone else have it this time. Again, I appreciate your thoughtfulness."

Notice that I am focusing on gratitude, and positive statements.

Write out a few possible responses that come from your heart center and that honor your choice to focus your time on your own creative SPIRITED goals. Now you will have a good response to requests that deprive you of your essential creative time.

Organizing Our Space

"Order is the shape upon which beauty depends."
PEARL S. BUCK

Saying "yes" to those things that nurture and support us is a habit well worth cultivating. We can open up space in our weekly schedule that will give us the time we need to follow our creative calling. But it is also essential that we have physical space to do our work. Some creative activities require specialized equipment like a kiln or a loom, while others may only need a small table at an outdoor café. Whether you have a fully equipped art studio or a plastic box under your bed, considering how your space contributes to your creative success will help you to create an environment that nurtures you and allows you to create with ease and grace.

For some of us, the challenge is finding a space that we can call our own, a place where we can leave our work out so that it is ready for us to pick up where we left off. Even a designated corner can give us the sense of support that is needed to develop our creative plans. Creating an organized environment conducive to both dreaming and working supports your success. This space also holds the tools that you need to create.

Here are some of the factors you might consider for a workspace:

- Lighting

- Bookshelves

- Tables

- Chairs

- Ventilation

- Temperature control

- View/ Nature

- Inspiration boards.

- Wall space

- Storage

- Accessibility

- Water source/ Sink

- Drainage/ Disposal

Several years ago, during a teleconference coaching session that I was facilitating, the group was focusing on how their space supported their particular creative work. We were talking about our desks and about organizing our writing area. As I listened to each of my clients, I became acutely aware that the office chair that I was sitting in at my desk had been broken for some time. It was so awkward to sit in. It was actually distracting me during my coaching sessions. I had been using the chair even though I had several other choices of chairs available to use. Changing chairs was a simple thing to do and it made a significant difference in my ability to do my creativity coaching.

Assessing Your Space

Take a good look at your creative space. Do you have what you need to create? Ask yourself:

1. Do I have the space I need to follow my creative pursuits? If not, what changes do I need to make?

2. How can I make my creative place into a sacred space that is honored by my significant others?

3. What changes can I make to my space that will make a difference in the way I work?

4. What change will support me the most in accomplishing my current project?

Our Creative Stuff

"Every master knows that the material teaches the artist."

Ilya Ehrenberg

Do you have the materials you need to explore your passionate creative urges? Some people dream of following a creative urge, but never support themselves with the materials they need to create. Other creative people get stuck in the phase of acquiring and stockpiling the materials but never get to the point of actually using them.

As creative people, we may find ourselves drowning in the vastness of our collection of supplies. We can see the creative potential in each item whether it is a bottle of acrylic paint or bits of scrap cardboard. Accruing materials is a part of the creative process, yet, we can sabotage ourselves by overdoing it. When we become tenders of the stuff, we can find that there is so much stuff to store that we don't have room to create. Or we can't actually find what we need or we spend more time organizing our studio than making things! When this is the case, our energy may become stagnant and we experience a lack of flow. We may feel guilty when we don't have the time to use all that we have, or we might feel overwhelmed.

How can we simplify and create a space that works optimally? Here are some suggestions for clearing away some of the excess:

- Have a studio clean-out sale

- Donate supplies to the local schools

- Donate materials to a youth group like the Girl Scouts, or the Boys and Girls Club

- Find out if you have an "Art from Scrap" program locally that recycles materials for the schools

- Hold a free workshop for your community. Put out a generous supply of odd-lot materials and invite them all to make something

SHINE ON

Relationship to Materials

To focus your awareness on your relationship to your materials, answer the following:

1. Do I have the materials that I need to create what I have been envisioning?

2. If not, what do I need so that I can move to the next level of success?

3. Are my materials overwhelming or distracting me? How can I clarify just what I need?

SPIRAL ACTIVITY

An Altar of Creativity

Many creative people have found ways to bring their dreams to life in a minimum of space. The more important factor is the mental, spiritual and emotional honoring of the space as a place that is of the utmost importance to the creative process. Setting up a small altar or display of tokens that speak to you at a deep level is one way of dedicating your space.

You will need:
The spiral page at the end of this chapter
A box large enough to hold the spiral
Objects and tokens that hold meaning for you

Dedicate your space with a small altar of sacred tokens that hold special meaning for you. Copy the large spiral image onto a piece of paper and place it in the bottom of a box. Arrange objects that hold significance for you in the box to let them influence your spirit. You may want to arrange the items according to their meaning, by placing the most powerful one in the center and the other objects around the central token. Place the altar in your workspace where you can easily view it and where others will see it as well. This may be a good spot to keep your Affirmation Cards, your Creativity Cards, and your Spiral Cards.

AFFIRMATION

Real Time and Space

"The work that is real for me is the work that originates in my own head and is created with my own hands. I am at peace with my relationship with time, space and materials."

CREATE YOUR OWN REAL AFFIRMATION

Chapter Six

Authentic:
Moving Toward Our
Individual Dream

"This above all, to thine own self be true, for
it must follow as dost the night the day,
thou canst not then be false to any man."

WILLIAM SHAKESPEARE

E ach of us has the inner wisdom to create a rich life that
is a unique expression of our individual spirit. As we
have been making our way through the spiral activities, we
have been discovering and clarifying who we are and how
we want to grow into our expanded vision of our self. At
every step of the way, we have had to check in with our body
sensations and our inner guidance to determine what is right
for us. We are uncovering our authentic self, a combination
of our spirit, passions, and intuitive powers.

In the fields of psychology and art "authenticity" refers to
living your life according to your own inner guide. It means
being faithful to yourself, using your own inner compass and
not looking to outside sources to define you. You could say
that authenticity is the degree to which someone is true to
their own personal spirit and how well they resist outside

influences. Authenticity carries with it a sense of honest sincerity. Authenticity, intuition, and creativity go hand in hand. Our creative nature allows us to be comfortable with our own inner wisdom rather than accepting outside expectations of what is right for us.

In his book *The Exquisite Risk: Daring to Live an Authentic Life* Mark Nepo writes about living from an "original presence." He says, "Given the chance, that place inside will speak to each of us."

Authenticity is essential for wellbeing. It contributes to our vitality, self-esteem, confidence, and ability to cope. Satisfaction—that elusive state of being that the Rolling Stones sang about in the '70s—is what we get when we are living authentically. When we are working from our soul center and are ecstatic about what we are doing, it becomes obvious to everyone around us that we are in the zone of living authentically.

⌇⌇

SHINE ON

What Does "Authentic" Mean to You?

Here are a few things that have come up in my workshops. Do any of these resonate with you? Pick the top three that seem to fit with your sense of what authentic means to you. Describe how they feel and how they show up in the work that you do. Are there any words or phrases here that just *don't* seem to fit? Write about them. What do they mean to you? Are there other things that came up for you when thinking about authenticity that are not here?

In the Zone	Veritable
Original	Genuine
Unmasked	Indigenous
Honorable	Trustworthy
True to self	Real
Honest	Integrity
Inner Voice	Sensitive
Inner-directed	Connected to your higher self

Why do so many creative people experience challenges when striving to work authentically? For one thing, we are living at a time when our field of influence has expanded to include pretty much the entire planet. Our ability to easily access information, images, and ideas from around the globe means that we have a bigger job to do filtering through all of the input we get on a daily basis. In the past, we consciously knew that those people and organizations that are closest to us including parents, family, friends, school, job, and religion could have a strong influence on our choices. In today's culture of worldwide connection, our circles of influence are constantly expanding.

When I was growing up and attending Catholic school, I thought that my ultimate goal was to get an "A" and go to heaven. I was driven by outside rewards, defining achievement by grades and certificates. As an adult, I had to discover my true, authentic guides and learn to listen to my own authority.

Eventually, I came up with a new paradigm to help me past my years of striving for the outside recognition of the "A." This linear way of thinking didn't fit my inner spirit, so I tweaked my focus to how I want to Be (B) and how I want to See (C). The letter "A" now stands for awareness and authenticity. These new "ABCs" help me to be in tune with my authentic self.

SHINE ON

Authenticity

Look through the following questions. Read each one out loud. Pay close attention to your body as you use these questions as writing prompts to explore your connection with your authenticity.

1. How do I know I am living authentically?

2. What does it feel like to be acting on an authentic choice?

3. When do I feel most authentic?

4. How do I nurture my authenticity?

5. What gets in the way of my living an authentic life?

6. What is the most significant outside voice that influences the choices I make?

7. What is the most supportive, helpful voice that I hear?

8. What is the most destructive outside influence that I have to deal with?

9. What would it take for me to disengage with that person or group?

10. How does making authentic choices contribute to my feelings of satisfaction and fulfillment?

Freedom and Structure

"There is no need to run outside for better seeing,
Nor to peer from a window.
Rather, abide at the center of your being;
For the more you leave it, the less you learn.
Search your heart and see
If he is wise who take each turn:
The way to do is to be."

LAO TSU

As the days glide from sunrise to sunset, we may find ourselves adrift in a sea of ideas, urgings and dabblings. So often, creative people are attracted to many different things at once. We want to make art, write a book, teach classes, feed our soul with gardening, take workshops, and begin a dozen other new endeavors each day that seem interesting and spark our attention. It's this capacity for imagining the possibilities that makes us feel so alive.

We also feel alive and successful when we can zero in on something, give it our focus, and take our idea to completion. Completing the full cycle from inspiration to installation, we experience a sense of joy and fullness that becomes the sweet rhythm of our days. When we spiral inward and listen carefully to our heart and spirit we begin to create a vision of what we want to create. Then, while we are endeavoring to express our vision, we sometimes find ourselves doing a crazy dance between not wanting to be tethered by outside influences and needing some kind of structure.

Let's talk about this dance a bit more. On the one hand, we want the freedom to follow our intuition, to be open to inspiration, to be present to the moment, and to respond to those things that resonate with us. On the other hand, we know that structure is important in order for us to organize ourselves and to build results. We have the tools that help us to set goals and make plans, but we may still find structure a difficult concept.

When I dreamed of getting my book on creative knitting published, I hired a creativity coach. He talked to me about structuring my time and he used the word "discipline." The first thing he suggested was to get up early every morning and write before I did anything else. There was so much about this advice that made me recoil on every level. I am not a morning person. I am more successful if I give myself time to adjust to the day. I have never, ever been able to sustain a practice of getting up extra early to do anything.

The word "discipline" sent me into an emotional tailspin as I thought of my father's idea of parenting through discipline, which occasionally involved spanking with a leather belt. I had attended Catholic school where discipline was used to create absolute obedience and uniformity, which I hated. I couldn't conceive of discipline as being connected to creativity in any way.

I wrote a rant about what discipline meant to me. I wrote about how I felt about early morning writing sessions. I fussed and fumed. And then I calmed down and tried to find the essence of what was being suggested and translate it into something I could work with.

I set a daily writing schedule at the decent hour of nine a.m. I wrote out my SPIRITED goal and created a SASSIE plan. I created a timeline and committed to sitting and writing for one hour, five days a week. I used a ritual to get me started: Sit down with pad and pen, tea in mug. Light a candle, set a timer, and start writing. Continue for twenty minutes. When the timer went off, I read what I wrote and reset the timer for the next forty minutes and went from there. I called this my routine.

With that kind of structure, I made sizable advances in my book. I began to make connections more easily. I found I could get into the writing zone more quickly. I saw the results and was inspired, encouraged, and motivated. I realized that this daily writing structure moved me forward in a way that my former write-when-I-felt-like-it style of approaching my book never had.

I was able to see that doing the work, consistently, daily, with focus, produced results. I never felt it was interfering with my free flow of creativity. Actually, just the opposite; I found myself making connections easily and often. I felt the joy of feeling the flow of ideas all day long and the satisfaction of recording those ideas regularly.

SHINE ON

Structure

Write about your relationship with structure or discipline. Let these prompts guide you to your authentic thoughts and feelings about the way that you approach your creative work.

1. In my creative life, what role does freedom play?

2. What role does discipline play?

3. How do they interact?

4. What helps me to focus?

5. How does discipline support my progress in my work?

6. What kinds of structures work for me?

7. How can I create a structure that supports me and still feel spontaneous and free?

Focus

"When you stay focused and keep a commitment you create momentum, and momentum creates momentum."
RICH FETTKE

The red-tailed hawk that lives in our valley had just landed on a branch of the giant eucalyptus tree on the opposite hill. My husband pointed his newly acquired binoculars at the tree and whispered in hushed tones of pure awe, "Wow! Look at that magnificent bird. He's got something in his talons."

Excitedly, he passed me the binoculars. I put them to my eyes, but I was disappointed that I couldn't see the hawk, or even the branch of the tree. Everything was out of focus. I was missing out on the wonderful nature show unfolding in front of me. But then, by focusing the binoculars to my individual way of seeing, everything changed. I was able to see clearly and enjoy the amazing display as the hawk took flight.

As creative people, we often find that our goals and intentions get harder and harder to see clearly as we try to balance all of the different elements of our busy lives. How can we focus in on what is important to us, and on our goals and intentions?

Each of the exercises in this book has been helping you to clearly see your true creative nature. You have been clarifying who you are, what you value, and how you want to be in the world. You have been continually spiraling back around to your individual spirit, to incorporate your strengths and values; to your passion, in order to include what makes you happy and fuels you; and to your intuition, to confirm your inner wisdom. You have learned how to create supportive strategies, cultivate nurturing habits and use organizing tools to move you forward toward your dreams.

Now you can synthesize all that you have learned to create a statement of purpose that will guide you and keep you on track.

～⤨～

SHINE ON

Write a Declaration of Creative Individuality

Look over all of the writing that you have been doing as you completed the Shine On exercises in the previous chapters. Now you can use your insights to help you form a declaration statement that you can use to focus your energy and guide you toward expressing your authentic voice.

Look at the questions and use them as prompts to write a positive statement of your creative individuality. The questions are purposely designed to give you a variety of different ways to approach the core essence of who you are and what it is you want to express in the world.

Take your time. Let the statements weave together in their own natural way. Some will organically go together and some will stand on their own. There is no preset order, only your sense of what feels right. Start you sentences with "I" and use positive words with emotional impact to add power to your statements.

1. What is important to me? Precious? Sacred? Essential?

2. What do I want to stand for? What is the essence of what I want to share with the world?

3. What is my creative activity about? What is my soul longing to express?

4. What fundamental belief fuels my work with spirit and gives me a reason to create?

5. What is my personal style of working? What brings me joy and what detracts from it?

6. What do I want to express more of?

7. What do I want to be identified by?

8. How do I express my uniqueness?

9. What do I hear my inner voice wanting to shout out?

10. What do I dream myself to be?

11. What do I place my faith in?

12. What gives me hope? Peace? Joy?

Once you have written a declaration that feels wonderful to you, print it out. Frame it and hang it in a place of honor. Read it often. Let it become an affirmation of your authentic individuality. Use it to focus your attention and energy when life gets busy and distracting.

Here is one of the many declarations that I have written over the years:

"I am committed to studying, practicing, and supporting creative thought and action in the world by fostering and witnessing the individual process of accessing the natural, authentic knowing inside as a center point for a spirited, passionate, and joyously creative life. I am passionate about creating quality art work; inspiring creativity in others; cultivating a sense of exploration, openness, and discovery; sharing my passion for creative textile processes; and contributing to my community through my art and experience."

Claiming Our Inner Authority

"Obstacles are opportunities for
us to grow and learn.
That is how we become empowered.
You've got to jump off cliffs all the time and
build your wings on the way down."
RAY BRADBURY

As we strive to live more and more authentically we allow ourselves to no longer rely on outside sources for guidance, approval, or permission. We claim our power and make our decisions based on our own inner wisdom. We take full responsibility for our creative actions. We face the unknown bringing our awareness to what we are thinking and feeling about the risks that lie ahead.

As we enter the unknown, we may discover that we have inner guardians standing at the ready to protect us from venturing too far off the familiar path. These guardians may feel like fear or something quite a bit more like a loving parent who believes it is their job to hold us back from harm. We find that we must give ourselves permission to move ahead toward our dreams.

As a parent, I signed many permission slips for my three kids as they adventured their way through an outdoor education-oriented middle school. Some of these requests tested me to my very soul: they asked me not only to allow my child to go white water river rafting, but to do so with the full knowledge that they might fall out of the boat and be in serious danger or even die. I gave my permission for them to sleep in snow, bicycle in rain, kayak in the ocean, and travel by plane, train, boat, and horse. I once signed a permission slip for my son to go to India, even though the form delineated various possible causes of injury or death, including being trampled by an elephant or bitten by wild dogs.

Because I knew that each situation would provide amazing experiences for my child, I realized that I could not stand in their way. My instinct to protect them had to be tempered by my faith in their abilities and the value of these exciting kinds of learning opportunities. The loving thing to do was to open the door and provide my blessing.

If you imagine there is a part of you that wants to protect you like a parent would protect a child, you can direct that energy and love by giving yourself permission to take risks and reach past your comfort zone to experience amazing new adventures.

SHINE ON

What Do You Need to Give Yourself Permission For?

Create a safe and comfortable space in which you can open a dialogue with your inner guardians. Recognize that they are motivated by love, even when they are afraid to let you grow. Listen to their voices with patience. They might be stuck on the possible dangers that they perceive in change. Let them know that you are ready, willing, and able to take on the risk of living your spirited life. Reassure them that you have the faith to take each step along the way. Ask them to support you as you explore and experiment, holding the door open for you to discover what you need to expand.

Record your dialogue in your journal. After you have exchanged your thoughts and feelings with your inner guardians, write them a thank-you letter letting them know that you appreciate their blessings and that you honor their role in your creative journey.

CREATE TO RELATE

Permission Slip

Having a physical permission slip available for our creative adventure gives us the opportunity to check in with our authentic authority each time we sense restriction, hesitation, fear, doubt, or our own overbearing inner parent. Create a permission slip for yourself. You can use the form provided or make your own. Be sure that it includes a place for your signature and the date.

I, _____

give myself permission to _____

_____

_____

_____

_____

I understand that I may not actually know what the end result will be when I begin. I am willing to risk not knowing so that I can find my own original, authentic expression.

Signed _____

Date _____

Perfectionism

"The principle mark of genius is not perfection but originality, the opening of new frontiers."
ARTHUR KOESTLER

Our focused awareness has taken us from spiraling our attention inward and claiming our authentic voice to spiraling outward to express our individuality in the world. Along the way, we have become familiar with the whole range of thoughts, emotions, and bodily sensations that are distinctly ours. We have clarified our unique spirit; identified our passionate fuel; embraced and accepted our fears and doubts; claimed our intuitive powers; and given ourselves permission to venture out of our comfort zones.

Now we are bringing our intentions into being, applying the tools we have learned, and stepping into the creative unknown to make our imagined goals become real. Doing our creative work is inherently a messy business. Some of what we do will be gorgeously successful; some of what we do will lead us to new possibilities: and some of what we do will teach us about what *not* to do next time. Only a small fraction of what we do will ever reach the realm of perfection.

Creativity and perfection serve two distinctly opposite purposes. We can only perfect those processes that we know expertly. This means that perfection only comes when there are no new discoveries to be made, no new skills or techniques to learn, and no new decisions to be made. The path is set. Familiarity replaces risk. Repetition brings greater skill. Perfection extends the end of the creative process by prolonged awareness of the creative task.

Perfection is hosted in the known, creativity in the unknown. Perfection is a judgment call that we either make ourselves, or we let an authority outside ourselves define. When we are claiming our authenticity, we can bring our awareness to our personal standards for our finished creations and to our relationship to the outside standards that we encounter in our creative fields.

SHINE ON

Perfectionism

Perfectionism can deter us from our creative purpose, especially when we hold onto standards for our work that are impossible to reach or we cultivate the habit of judging our work at every step of the creative process. Take time to focus on your thoughts about perfection. Write about what perfection means to you. Use the prompts to get your thoughts flowing.

1. What place does perfection have in my creative life?

2. If perfection means that something is free of flaws, how do I know when that is true for my creation?

3. How do I create a relationship between perfection and creativity?

CREATE TO RELATE

Interview with Perfection and Creativity

Imagine that you are a TV talk show host and you have invited both your personal perfection and your creativity to be guests on the show. Prepare questions for them that will help to reveal their deepest secrets.

Imagine how they would look when they appear on your show. Ask them your questions and listen while they answer. Write it all down as if it were a script or screenplay, including stage notes, costuming, lighting, and any other details that help to bring out the nature of your relationship with perfection and creativity.

Here is what this might look like:

"Ladies and gentlemen, our first guest is here from all the way back in my childhood, always on time and looking fabulous. Let's give a warm welcome to Perfection!"

Perfection enters wearing a crisp blouse with a designer jacket over a pencil skirt with black pumps. Her hair is stylishly cut, and her makeup is light but effective. She walks over to the couch, smiles at the audience, and tucks her skirt under as she sits gracefully down and places her manicured hands in her lap.

"Perfection, how is your new project coming along?"

Now it's your turn to write out an interview scenario. Have fun with your script. The more details, the better!

SPIRAL ACTIVITY

Create an Authentic Compass

When we claim our inner authority, we become more and more comfortable with turning inward for the direction we need as we encounter questions, challenges, and obstacles in our creative adventures. Creating this authentic compass helps to remind us to listen to our own wise voice and to trust our authentic knowing.

You will need:

A piece of cardboard 12' x 12"

A spiral page

Colored markers

Scissors

A two-pronged fastener

Cut the spiral out in a large circle. In the center of the spiral, write "Passion. Love. Heart." Then write "Intuition, Inner Wisdom, Inner Knowing, and Authentic Self" along the spiral, starting from the center and working your way outward. Near the opening of the spiral, write, "Spirit."

Poke a hole in the middle of the cardboard. Press the fastener through the center of the spiral and the cardboard and press back the prongs to attach them together. Check to make sure that the spiral can spin freely. In the four corners of the cardboard, outside of the spiral write: "Creative Project. Home. Work. Relationships."

To use your compass: When you have a question or a decision to make, turn the opening of the spiral so that it faces the appropriate corner. For example, if you are not sure what your next step should be in a creative project, spin the spiral so that the opening of the spiral, where you've written "Spirit," would be facing the corner where you wrote, "Creative Project."

Take a deep breath and call to mind the question or decision. Look at your compass to remind you to allow this metaphoric alignment to inform you. Follow the spiral pathway from Spirit, through Intuition and Authenticity, to your Passionate love center. Listen deeply. Take as much time as you need to let the answers come to you. Check in with your body. Place the compass in a spot where it will remind you of your powerful authentic wisdom.

This kind of visual compass supports our intuitive ways of knowing. Like a vision board or altar, the compass acts to activate our intuitive wisdom. Unlike the spinner in a board game, the answers are not instantaneous. We may need to practice patience as we allow the answer to unfold.

AFFIRMATION

I Am Authentic

"What a joy it is to be able to claim my originality. I put my seal of approval on my creative endeavors and announce that they are the genuine, bona fide work of my own hands. I proclaim that I am a trustworthy source for inspired work. I give myself permission to flounder, to explore, and to dream. I trust my inner wisdom to guide me."

CREATE YOUR OWN AUTHENTIC AFFIRMATION

Chapter Seven

Living Your Spirited, Creative Life

"We have learned so much
There still remains much to learn.
We are not going in circles,
we are going upwards,
The path is spiral;
we have already climbed many steps."

HERMANN HESSE IN *SIDDHARTHA*

I n choosing awareness and claiming our authenticity, we take the risk. We work from our unique spirit in order to experience the feelings associated with those sparkling, spiraling light trails against the darkness of the night sky. Every choice we make is an opportunity for us to center in our passionate self and to project our creative intentions out into the real world. The greater spiral is made up of days, months, and years. The daily spiraling happens with each breath, each thought, and each choice.

Jack Canfield begins his book *The Success Principles: How to Get from Where You Are to Where You Want to Be* by establishing that we are responsible for the choices we make and the life we experience. He tells us that we have to take 100 percent responsibility for our thoughts,

157

emotions, and reactions to everything that we encounter in our life.

I remember hearing Jack speak one evening here in Santa Barbara. I was so excited that he was speaking locally, since I had learned so much from his writing. I remember him saying that even our self-criticisms are motivated by love and that our process for transforming those thoughts also involved love. This simple truth is so very powerful. Simply put, we can choose love.

This is why we want to shine a light on our individual spirit, passion, and intuition. When we know who we are and how we want to be in the world, we have a basis for choosing the thoughts, feelings, and actions that serve to promote our highest well-being. This doesn't mean that we won't have thoughts or feelings of self-doubt, limitation, judgment, criticism, or complaints. We continue to be whole beings with a full range of choices. The key is that we know we have a choice to have well-being and that we can choose to see even our most limiting thoughts through the eyes of love. We are developing the self-awareness and tools to help us to choose what nourishes us. We can choose to bring love to every situation.

⁂

SHINE ON

Daily Choices

What thoughts, feelings, and actions do you want to choose? Look back over all of the work you have done identifying what it is you value, what feels right to you, and what you love.

Name five different situations that you encounter on a regular basis that challenge you in some way. Write out a statement of what you want to choose for yourself in each situation.

"When this happens: I choose...."

Start with just one of these circumstances and bring your awareness to your choice each time you are in that place. Gently remind yourself of the choice that you want to make, and practice until the choice becomes natural. Then you can tackle another situation and repeat the process.

Example: Whenever I'm in the grocery store, I look for the shortest checkout line to make my way out of the store as quickly as possible. Inevitably, I find myself in line with someone who has some reason for taking the longest possible time to check out. Perhaps they have dozens of coupons, which they forgot to give the checkout clerk, but insist on redeeming or they write a check that requires the manager's approval—and the manager is on break.

I could choose to become impatient, angry, and frustrated. I could choose to think about how important my time is and how it is being squandered. I could choose to look around and see how many people have checked out before me, even though they were in lines longer than mine, and feel cheated. In fact, I have thought all of those things and felt incredibly upset more times than I care to report here.

If I were to choose this as my circumstance to shine on, I would write out a statement like this: "While waiting in the checkout line of any grocery store, no matter how long it takes to check out, I choose patience, compassion, curiosity and gratitude."

I could elaborate further: "I choose to radiate that patience and compassion to everyone in line with me. I choose to look around with curious eyes and to wonder at the gifts that this store holds for me. I choose to feel grateful for the opportunity to be able to come to this place and exchange money for so many wonderful things to eat and use that make my life comfortable, fun, and enjoyable.

There is a physical shift in energy when we choose to see our situation through our choice of love and gratitude. A sense of calm curiosity replaces impatience. We are able to feel our creative flow in any circumstance. Essentially we've just created an affirmation for ourselves.

Now it's your turn. What do you choose? Feel free to elaborate. Does what you wrote work as an affirmation? If so you may want to create a card to keep in your pocket, bag, car, or briefcase so you have this reminder with you while you are on the go.

Gratitude

"The essence of all beautiful art, all great art, is gratitude."
FRIEDRICH NIETZSCHE

Choosing gratitude is a simple, yet powerful tool that we can use to support our creative life. When we take time to bring our awareness to all of the good in our life and feel thankful, it opens up our hearts, clearing a path that allows our inner wisdom to flow freely. Gratitude opens us up to new possibilities as we center ourselves in appreciation for each gift that life has to give us. Gratitude aligns our thoughts and feelings with our love center and our intuition, so that our creative powers are fired up and ready to go. That's why, when we set an intention, we express gratitude for receiving what it is we are asking for. Gratitude opens the way for our good to come in.

SHINE ON

Journal Your Gratitude

Bringing our awareness to those things that we are thankful for shifts our energy and places us in alignment body, mind, heart, and spirit. Writing out what you are grateful for can become a simple way to power up. Here are three exercises for cultivating a daily choice of gratitude.

1. Create a gratitude practice by listing at least five things that you are grateful for at the end of each day.

2. Create your master list. Write out as many things as you can think of that you are grateful for. For many of us, this will include our loved ones and aspects of our home and work. Rather than listing "family" write out the name of each person in your life that you are grateful for. Spell out all of the small things that you love about your home. Use each of your senses. Do you love the smell of the fire in the fireplace? Are you grateful for the sounds of the birds in the morning outside of your kitchen window? Put it all down to create your master list. You may want to keep this private, or you may want to post it somewhere you will see it often.

3. Supersize it! I love doing this as a way of shifting my energy when I'm in a funk or stuck in my own spiral of negative thinking. Without thinking too much, quickly make a list of 100 things you are grateful for. You can use anything

on your master list and then really tune in to the moment. Look around. Listen. Sniff. Become aware of the sensations you are feeling right now. Write everything that comes to you at that moment that infuses you with a feeling of being alive. Nothing is too small. Actually, the tiny little details are what make this such a good exercise.

After you have written down fifty things that you are grateful for, the next fifty may require you to look a little deeper. Keep going! When you are done check in with your body to find the ways in which this exercise has shifted your energy.

Beauty

"When we dwell in the senses, we downshift from a rushed pace into the slower pace of organic life. Emotions and mind come into resonance with the deep rhythms of the body, promoting integration and well-being. We notice the beauty around us, and we use it to grow."

BONNIE GOLD BELL

Have you ever noticed how your body reacts in the presence of something truly beautiful? I have actually felt like running toward something I find beauty in, as if it had a magnetic force drawing me to it. Beauty urges us to respond, to take it in visually, physically, and spiritually. We have a physical reaction when we encounter beauty and a very personal connection to that which we deem beautiful. We find ourselves quieted with appreciation, and at the same time, animated with energy. We feel a sense of awe and wonder.

We drink in the smells and sounds; we bathe in the color and light; we lean into the shapes and lines. We celebrate our good fortune at having had the encounter and we submit ourselves so that this beauty will impress itself on our minds and hearts, so that we can prolong our enjoyment. We feel transformed and renewed.

Whether we are appreciating something exquisite from nature or something crafted by human hands, we can feel a real release of stress, doubt, fear and judgment when we surrender to beauty. Bringing our awareness to the beauty in our lives helps us to be present to our surroundings, to feel joyfully uplifted, to inspire hope, and to appreciate even the smallest bits of color and texture that make our hearts sing. This allows our creative energy to flow freely.

We drop all need to judge as we find ourselves immersed in grace. We become devoid of criticism and open to letting the beauty fill us. Who watches a beautiful sunset into the ocean and determines that one beam of color is just not up to par, or that the ocean is not the right shade of blue? We feel ourselves rise up to meet the beauty and at the same time we feel humbled in its presence.

How can we tune into our physical sense of beauty in our day-to-day lives? Here are some suggestions to get you started:

> Bring natural beauty into your home and work space by displaying flowers, stones, twigs, feathers, or photos of natural scenarios that make you feel uplifted.

> Listen daily to the sounds you love, whether you include the croaking of frogs or your favorite symphony.

Bring your awareness to sensations on your skin, from the warmth of the sun to the cool crispness of clean sheets.

Eat slowly and consciously, especially when enjoying foods that you love. Take in the aromas, the colors, and the textures as well as all of the flavors.

Fill your spaces with scents from flowers, candles, oils, or the aroma of baked goods. Notice the way that the fragrances rejuvenate your whole sensory system.

SHINE ON

Practice Beauty

"Dwell on the beauty of life.
Watch the stars, and see yourself
running with them."
MARCUS AURELIUS

Take in the beauty that surrounds you. Think about ways you can incorporate more beauty into your daily life. Do you need to do something differently? Go somewhere new? What beauty can you find without changing anything except your awareness of beauty? Write about your experiences with beauty.

Wabi Sabi

"Ring the bell that still can ring
Forget your perfect offering
There is a crack in everything
That's how the Light gets in."

LEONARD COHEN

Years ago, my friend Jill introduced me to the concept of Wabi Sabi. I had been to Kyoto to study at the Kawashima Textile School and I think that she assumed I was familiar with this type of aesthetic. My style certainly was very much in tune with Wabi Sabi, so when I finally learned more about it, I felt like I was coming home. Jill lent me her copy of Leonard Koren's book *Wabi Sabi for Artists, Designers, Poets & Philosophers* and there I found a philosophy rooted in Taoism and Chinese Zen Buddhism that fits my own philosophy of creativity.

The concept of Wabi Sabi comes from the art of tea ceremony and shares the ideals of simplicity, naturalness, and an acceptance of the wholeness of life. Wabi has been associated with an inward spiritual path, and Sabi with the outward signs of a life that is rooted in accepting the inevitable bitter-sweetness that accompanies the tension of the opposites.

In his book, Koren describes a sense of beauty as well as a way of being. He talks about the beauty of things that are imperfect, impermanent, and incomplete. He suggests an intuitive approach to beauty that includes embracing the mysterious and accidental along with the weathering effects of all of the natural elements. Wabi Sabi invites us to look closely and to shine a light on every bit of life no matter how insignificant it seems to discover what may have been missed.

The Wabi Sabi principles as I see them, fit well with our spiral into creativity. We are reminded to appreciate each step of our learning journey and to open our perspective on beauty, and on life, by accepting the natural processes. The creative process also has an inherent natural rhythm and requires us to make peace with imperfection. The principles of Wabi Sabi remind us that creativity is not perfection because it focuses on acceptance.

SHINE ON

Wabi Sabi

Wabi Sabi is both a philosophy and a style. You have been shining a light on your authentic way of being and creating. You may be just beginning to explore how you want to express your authentic voice, or you may already have a signature style. This is another way to explore your "ness" that we introduced in Chapter One.

Here are a few more of the aesthetic concepts associated with Wabi Sabi: rustic, earthy, unpretentious, murky, crude, circular, organic, soft, intimate, vague shapes and edges, mysterious and elusive, hard to define, inconspicuous, imperfect, accidental, tarnish, rust, stain, warping, shrinking, shriveling, cracking, peeling.

Does any of this resonate with your creative style? Write about what jives with the way you work and what does not. This is just one approach to creating. Can you generate a list of words that fit your style? Do you have some way of working that doesn't depend on materials but on the way that you approach the creative process?

Joy

"Happiness is when what you think, what
you say, and what you do are in harmony."
Mahatma Gandhi

Living our spirited creative life allows us to choose the feelings that we want to focus on, cultivate and share. Choosing joy seems like it would be a naturally good idea. We might think that we would automatically gravitate toward nurturing joy on a day-to-day basis. Yet, even feeling joyful may take some practice as we move through the creative process.

Whether writing a book, selling a painting, performing on stage, or planting a garden, our goals have deep and serious meaning for us. We may get caught up in all of the feelings that come with deadlines and setbacks or with facing our very real fears and doubts. We may need to remind ourselves to lighten up, breathe, and allow the flow by not taking everything so seriously. We can spiral back to our passions and allow our joy to fuel us.

Anxiety and worry come from our automatic negative thoughts. Sometimes we need help to change those thoughts into more positive ones. We have discovered that affirmations are a useful tool.

When my kids were growing up on our wooded acre in Santa Barbara, we named our property "The Happy Valley." We had a family nighttime routine that included gathering on someone's bed and then sharing our "happiest things." We would all pile onto the chosen bed and take turns sharing two things: What our happiest thing was from the day, and then, what we thought might be our happiest thing for tomorrow. That way, we went to sleep feeling joyful and anticipating our good feelings to come.

Joy is a sensual experience. Tune into your senses as you weave together your passion, gratitude, and beauty practices. These are powerful mood-shifters and can easily light up your day.

Use all that you have discovered during your Shine On writing exercises to help you to surround yourself with ways to tune into joy.

One simple way to diffuse feelings of worry and switch to new energy is by turning to music. One of my favorite songs is "Don't Worry, Be Happy" by Bobbie McFerrin. The words and tune to this famous song are a terrific affirmation that is easy to remember. I downloaded this song to my computer and phone so I can listen to it while I'm at home or in the car. What music do you like to use to lift your spirits and shift your energy? Let it get stuck in your head. Whistle along. How can you incorporate it into your daily routine?

During a particularly difficult time, my husband and I agreed to remind each other to focus on our happiness in each present moment. Having been a camp counselor in my youth, I immediately thought of the song lyrics, "If you're happy and you know it, clap your hands." We would start each day with a hardy clap before we even got out of bed and then would clap frequently throughout the day. This became our special way of supporting each other, and it never failed to make us smile. We still like to engage in random clapping from time to time.

There will be many occasions when we can lighten up by bringing a bit of humor into play. Using humor as a first approach to facing a difficulty or conflict diffuses the negative energy and allows creative solutions to surface. Having an optimistic outlook, enjoying a sense of humor, and having a good laugh support our creative connectivity and open us up to feeling deep joy.

I love the movie *Monsters Inc* in which the land of the monsters ends up being fueled by children's laughter. At first, the monsters tap into the energy generated by fear—but joy turns out to be the more sustainable choice. Laughter wins.

SHINE ON

Cultivating Joy

Developing a joy practice is a great tool for infusing us with positive energy. This is another way of looking at how our passion fuels us. Write out the answers to these questions and then create a toolbox of things that you can use in your joy practice.

1. How do you cultivate joy?

2. What makes you belly laugh?

3. How do you use humor as a catalyst?

4. Create a list of things that make you laugh.

5. What are your favorite jokes? What about You Tube videos? Music? Images? Memories?

Incorporate these into your joy practice. Feel free to borrow the practice of clapping your hands! Singing the song is great, too.

Cycles

*"It's important to do the work that
leads to our renewal, clarity and
inspiration and then remember to taste
it, experience it and let it flow."*

LINDA SACCOCCIO

Spiraling in. Spiraling out. Circling around, again and again. Managing the ups and downs, the ins and outs, the ebb and flow. The dynamic energetic flow of the spiral captures the essence of our spirited life. We are in motion. Recognizing the natural rhythm, accepting it and embracing it, is a full-time job for us. Letting go of any judgment of either our "ins" or our "outs," we have opportunity after opportunity to grow and expand. Do we judge our own exhale? Or the waves as they recede after crashing on the shore?

Our spirited, creative life reflects the natural cycles of birth, growth, death, and rebirth.

Our intuitive nature supports the cycles of the creative process as we conceive of new ideas and bring them into the real world. If we pay close attention to how we feel when we complete a particular project, we may be surprised by what we experience. Along with feelings of joy and accomplishment, we may feel a full range of emotions including sadness and a sense of loss. This can be confusing, especially if our project was a success, achieved acclaim, and was exhibited or sold. We might be tempted to push through this time and jump into something new. But taking the time to honor this integration phase of our creative endeavor gives us an opportunity for wholeness.

Being in tune with the cyclical nature of creative work helps us to embrace this time as a natural phase in our development. By letting the cycle come to completion and accepting the endings, we can enter into a time of rest. Completely embracing this down time and bringing our awareness inward, listening to our inner wisdom, we set the stage for the conception and birth of new ideas. We honor each phase of our projects from inspiration to installation, as well as the fertile time we need for integration and renewal.

SHINE ON

Creative Cycles

In Chapter Four, we looked at how our creative process follows the spiraling pathway from our intention to its installation and then to the time when we integrate all that we have learned.

Write about a time when you have completed a project. How did you experience the integration or "death" phase of the creative cycle?

Celebrating Our Creative Growth

"Celebrate what you want to see more of."
TOM PETERS

When we take a look outside and observe the drama of nature unfolding before us, we are reminded to bring awareness to the growth and expansion that is happening in our own creative life. How many of us plunge into our work each day without really noticing how much we've grown? Are you taking the fruits of your creative labor for granted?

Every now and then, we can stop and take stock of how far we have come along our creative path. When we record all that we dream of creating, achieving, developing, and manifesting, we can check on our creative growth and expansion as we move toward and beyond our goals. Then we can celebrate our successes and share our joy and satisfaction.

⤭

SHINE ON

Creative Growth

By bringing our awareness to our creative growth, we give ourselves an opportunity to feel the joy of living our passion. Use the following questions to take a survey of where you are at on your spiral of creativity:

1. How do you keep track of your creative growth?

2. What fruits of your work have you harvested?

3. How do you handle your down time?

4. How do you take care of yourself when you are tired? Or, not feeling well?

5. What do you do to re-energize?

6. To get motivated?

7. To get inspired?

8. To feel joy?

9. To beat the blues?

10. To push through a challenge?

11. To face an obstacle?

12. To move forward on a goal?

13. How do you celebrate your success?

Mastering the art of the spirited life means that we bring our awareness to the continual spiraling movement inherent in the creative process. We allow the spiral inward to help us claim our individual spirit, our passionate center, intuitive wisdom, and authentic powers.

We are continually spiraling outward to share our gifts with the world.

CREATE TO RELATE:

Weave a Dream Vessel

"Spiraling into the center
The center of the wheel,
Spiraling in to the center
The center of the wheel
I am the weaver
I am the woven one
I am the dreamer
I am the dream"

CHANT BY LORNA KOHLER

Manifesting your dreams is a process instigated by intention, fueled by passion, and supported by our habits, tools, and goals. With each of our daily choices, we weave the colorful cloth of our creative lives.

Weave a small dream vessel to use as an amulet that will remind you of your role as the weaver of your own life.

You will need:
A piece of sturdy cardboard two by three inches
Three yards of strong string.
Yarn, ribbons, or fabric strips. Choose colors and textures
that you love.
A large-eyed tapestry needle
Sharp scissors
A fork

CREATING THE LOOM

The loom provides the framework and supports your work as you are doing it. As you follow the directions that follow for creating a small cardboard loom, think about what tools, practices, and habits support you in your creative work. Also identify your biggest supporters are and what they offer you.

To create your loom, you will cut sturdy cardboard into a two by three-inch piece to use for weaving your dream vessel. With sharp scissors, cut half-inch slits in the edge of the top of the loom along the two-inch side. Evenly space the slits one-quarter inch apart. Repeat for the bottom. Be sure that you have the same number of slits on top and bottom.

WARPING YOUR LOOM

In weaving, the warp is made up of the threads that are wrapped onto a loom to provide a foundation for the work. They are your starting point and they become intricately woven into the whole cloth. While you wind your warp following the directions that follow, think about these questions: What are your core beliefs? What is essential in your life? What is your creative vision?

To begin warping your cardboard loom, tie the end of the string around the end tab created by the first slit. Bring the string down and place it in the bottom slit, and then continue to bring it up the back of the loom. Place the string in the first slit on the top. Now you will be working at the top of the loom. Pull the string across the bottom of the first slit and over to the bottom of the next slit. It should make a horizontal line parallel to the top of the loom.

Now continue by placing the string into the second slit and up and over the top. Pull it tight so that the string stays down in the slit as you continue the string down the backside of the loom. Continue through the next slit on the bottom and up to the top, making a continuous loop.

Place the string into the last slit where you had the string. This time enter the slit from the front, bringing it down in the back, then across and over to the bottom of the next slit on the back. You now see a horizontal line on the back, similar to the one you made on the front. Bring the string through that slit to the front to continue down, through the next bottom slit and back up to the top.

At this point, you should see a piece of string that goes across the front, at the bottom of the top slits, and one that does the same thing on the back of the top slits. As you wind the warp, the bars across will alternate back and front at the top. There are no bars at the bottom of the loom. Continue in this way, creating bars at the top as you wrap the string around the loom. When you finish, tie the end of the string around the last tab and make a knot. Cut the string leaving a four-inch tail.

WEAVING THE WEFT

In weaving the threads that go over and under the warp to create the rows of cloth are called the weft. Think of your creative "weft" as being your daily habits, connections, thoughts, and actions. They provide the color and texture to your life. The weft threads circle around the loom, weaving over and under our creative vision, building up the whole fabric of our lives.

Cut a piece of yarn about three feet long and thread it onto your tapestry needle. The tapestry needle acts as a shuttle for weaving. Beginning at the bottom edge, weave the tip of the needle over the first warp strand and under the next. Continue weaving over and under until you have woven across the front of the loom. Pull the needle and yarn through until there is just a four 4inch tail dangling out of the side you started on. Leave that there for now.

When you get to the other side, turn the loom and weave across the back repeating the over and under pattern. Continue to weave around the loom until you run out of yarn. Add in a new piece by overlapping the strands about an inch and just continue. Use the fork to pack down the threads so that they are tightly pressed toward the bottom. Keep weaving until the warp is completely covered. When you get to the top, it will become more difficult to squeeze the needle over the warp strings. Weave as much as you can to create a sturdy bag.

When you can't fit in any more weaving, stop and cut the weft even with the edge of the bag. Now you are going to take the bag off of the loom. Pull the top tabs, alternating the ones that have the bar in the front toward you, and the ones with the bar in back, away from you. As you do this, slip the weaving away from the loom.

You will see that you have created a complete little bag, woven around the cardboard. Push the weaving down toward the bottom, wiggling the bottom warp strands so that they come loose from the bottom of the loom. Pull the vessel off of the loom, and even out the weaving so it covers all of the warp strands. Your dream vessel is ready for a handle.

ROPE HANDLE

In order for us to "handle" all of the various activities in our lives, we need to create a balance. Think about the daily choices you make to support your creative wholeness.

Measure and cut pieces of yarn that are at least twice as long as the finished rope length that you desire. Using two or more strands of yarn held together, tie an overhand knot at the very end. Leave a couple of inches of space and then tie another over hand knot. Now you can open a space in the yarns between the two knots and slip the yarn under the leg of a chair or over a hook.

Begin twisting all of the strands together in your fingers, continuously going in the same direction. It doesn't matter which direction. Continue to twist the strands together moving back, until you have twisted the entire length of the yarn. The tighter the twist, the tighter the finished rope will be.

Holding tight to the twisted ends, fold the strands in half so that the ends in your fingers meet with the end that is under the chair leg. You will see that the rope begins twisting around itself. Carefully take the end out from the chair leg and tie an over-hand knot with both ends together. Straighten along the length of the rope.

Attach the rope handle to your bag by stitching it on to the sides. Use your favorite color yarn and the tapestry needle to secure the rope.

Place a token in your amulet bag that represents strength, joy, wisdom or whatever qualities you would like to cultivate and celebrate. This token could be something from nature, like a smooth stone or a small shell. It could be something that you have created or a symbol that holds meaning for you.

Hang your amulet bag near a mirror. Think of the tokens as you look into your reflection and visualize yourself as embodying those qualities. You may want to place a copy of the "Spiraling into the Center" chant nearby as well. Continue to learn to trust yourself and to give yourself permission to express your truth.

SPIRAL ACTIVITY

More Spiral Ideas

For this final spiral activity, I am sharing a variety of ideas for you to do using the spiral symbol. This first activity is designed to align your intuitive senses with feelings of prosperity. Money is a powerful symbol and a token that we are intimately familiar with as coins are a part of our daily life.

Create a money spiral to shine a light on thoughts of abundance and prosperity. The coins can symbolize actual money or they may symbolize the many blessings that you are grateful for having or that you wish to manifest. Don't forget to approach this with the same childlike wonder that you have practiced in the previous chapters.

You will need:
The spiral page at the end of this chapter
Miscellaneous coins

Dump out your change and line the coins up on the spiral. Play with the different coins to create different effects. You can assemble the coins according to size or value, or just pick them up and use them randomly. Lay your money spiral out on a table where you can see it and play with rearranging the coins. Stack the coins to make a three-dimensional pattern. You may want to lay the spiral page out on your dresser or side table, where you can play with the coins often. Let your money spiral energize your thoughts of blessings flowing in and out, creating abundance and prosperity.

Here are more ways to play with the spiral:

- Create natural spirals by cutting the peel off of an orange in a spiral. Hang it and let it dry. Enjoy the fragrance.

- Create an outdoor spiral for your yard or garden using stones, driftwood, shells, marbles, or tiles.

- Plant a variety of succulents or cactus in a spiral.

- Create spiral-decorated wrapping paper by stamping colorful spirals onto plain brown paper or recycled paper grocery bags.

- Create a disappearing spiral by painting water onto a hard surface using a paint brush, sponge, squeeze bottle, your finger, or a stick.

- You can create a temporary spiral just about anywhere. Create a large walking spiral or a small mediation spiral with water and watch it disappear.

- You can use almost anything to assemble a temporary spiral. You can create a spiral with your peas on your dinner plate or use your kid's Legos or bobby pins, candy, the condiments in a restaurant...

Now add your own ideas and keep the spiral play going! You may want to collect images of the spiral or objects with the spiral symbol on them. I have spirals scattered throughout my home, studio, patio and garden that serve to remind me of my own growth, expansion, and creative possibilities.

⟵◦⟶

You are continually transitioning into your next discovery, stretching and expanding into that which is yet to be. Mastering the art of a spirited life is not meant to be a destination or a state of completion. Mastering the art of a spirited life is a process of weaving together your beautiful, individual spirit, your passionate heart, and your intuitive understanding in order to authentically express your one-of-a-kind creative spark and make your amazing dreams into a real life that you love. Moment by moment, shine on!

⟵◦⟶

FROM MY JOURNAL

Going around, and around, and around, each revolution one step closer, one level higher, one degree wider, more full, more rich, more complete. Going around a little slower, a little wiser, stopping along the way to help out wherever I can, reflecting a bit more of the light the closer I get to it; taking it on; passing it on; saying no to the stuff that isn't about love or joy or creation; saying yes to the moment.

"Sell your cleverness and buy bewilderment," Rumi tells us. Today I am discombobulated. That is a good sign. Maybe tomorrow I will be truly bewildered. Anyone want to buy some cleverness? Going out of business sale. Liquidation sale. Discount prices. Oh here, just take it! I'm not in the market for cleverness anymore.

The space between the lines.
Reading between the lines,
spiraling between the lines,
lying between the lines
in a place where the lights are dim, the air is soft,
the hum of the universe is a sweet song.
The sense of oneness with those I love, who love me,
lies over me like a blanket.
Like a blankie
A dear, comfortable blankie.
Blank space.
Void.
Gap.
Spiraling between the lines.

BRECIA KRALOVIC-LOGAN

AFFIRMATION

Sustaining the Spiral in My Life Choices

"As I continue to grow and expand in every way I see myself full of healthy vitality, energized and free. I am continually growing into my personal potential, improving my connection with my body, heart, mind, and spirit. I am centered in love, acceptance, compassion, and joy. I feel a deep sense of satisfaction, abundance and community. I choose to see the beauty in my life, and I am grateful."

CREATE YOUR OWN LIFE CHOICES AFFIRMATION

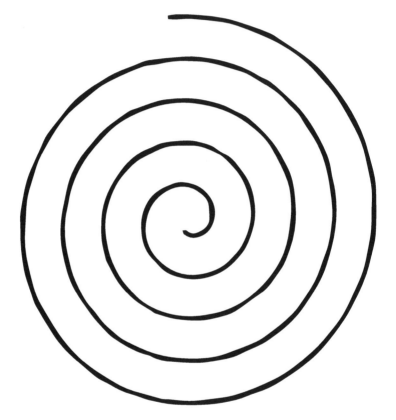

Acknowledgments

I am grateful for the mentorship and guidance of Eric Maisel, and Gail McMeekin. Both of these noted creativity experts and authors encouraged and inspired me to expand into my passion for sharing the creative process. I am grateful for the support of the Creativity Coaching Association and for the authentic connections I have made with other champions of creative living. I am especially thankful for everyone who participated in my workshops, attended my lectures, took my classes, and shared something of themselves in my coaching groups for completing the circle of experience.

The process of creating a book is truly a journey into the unknown. I am deeply grateful for the guidance of Ellen Reid, who supported me through each step of creation until this book became a reality. I also want to thank Lynda Rae for lending her creative hand and graphic expertise to bringing this book into being.

My heart overflows with gratitude for my husband, George and my adult children, Nikolas, Natasha, and Tatiana for their ever-present loving support and for each shining their spirits in their own way to light my path.

About the Author

Brecia Kralovic-Logan is a passionate champion of creativity who has spent the last 30 years helping people of all ages to embrace and express their unique individuality. Certified as a creativity coach, she helps her clients access their inner knowing, embrace their passions, and expand into their creative vision of joy and fulfillment.

Her zeal for color, texture, and movement has driven her own life as an artist and taken her from New York, to London, to Kyoto exploring various facets of the art world.

Applying her studies of Depth Psychology to her work as an arts educator, Kralovic-Logan teaches and lectures at international conferences, museums, colleges, and for arts organizations. She is the owner of pebble in the pond art studio in Santa Barbara, where she offers her national coaching services, writes, teaches and creates her award winning art.

Let's Keep in Touch!

I would love to meet with your group to share *The Spiral of Creativity* or lead a Creative Spiral Discovery Workshop. Please visit my websites for more resources on mastering the art of a spirited life and to see where I'll be and what I'm offering, so you can join the fun.

I teach all kinds of workshops focused on supporting your creative explorations and expression.

I also offer Creative Fire Circle and Creative Vision Circle group coaching by teleconference and in person. You may also want to join me for one of my fiber arts classes, workshops or retreats.

I would love to hear from you!

www.breciacreative.com

www.thespiralofcreativity.com

email: breciacreative@gmail.com

Made in the USA
Charleston, SC
08 April 2014